The Public Relations Writing Exercise Book

Sixth Edition

by

Bob J. Carrell
Professor Emeritus
University of Ollahoma

and

Doug A. Newsom
Professor
Texas Christian University

Wadsworth
Thomson Learning

Australia • Canada • Mexico • Singapore • Spain • United Kingdom • United States

ISBN 0-534-55640-x

For more information, contact
Wadsworth/Thomson Learning
10 Davis Drive
Belmont, CA 94002-3098
USA
http://www.wadsworth.com

International Headquarters
Thomson Learning
International Division
290 Harbor Drive, 2nd Floor
Stamford, CT 06902-7477
USA

UK/Europe/Middle East/South Africa
Thomson Learning
Berkshire House
168-173 High Holborn
London WC1V 7AA
United Kingdom

Asia
Thomson Learning
60 Albert Complex, #15-01
Singapore 189969

Canada
Nelson Thomson Learning
1120 Birchmount Road
Toronto, Ontario M1K 5G4
Canada

Contents

List of Examples

Preface

Ernest Hemingway once said that the first and most important thing of all for writers is to strip language clean, to lay it bare down to the bone. That advice is still valuable. You can learn about good writing by reading the works of good writers like Hemingway. And you can learn a lot from professors and from textbooks. But nothing substitutes for the actual practice of writing. Practice may not make you a perfect writer, but it can make you a better writer.

We continue to call this edition the *Public Relations Writing: Form & Style, Sixth Edition, Exercise Book* for two reasons. First, we wanted the title to be fully descriptive of the book's content and purpose. Second, we wanted the term *exercise* in the title to highlight the concept of writing practice. Like superb athletes, gifted writers practice, practice, practice.

This edition also helps you work independently on your writing or in concert with the ideas and skills to which you are introduced in a formal course. If you are presently enrolled in a public relations writing class, you may be using our sixth edition of *Public Relations Writing: Form & Style*. This book is coordinated with that text. We hope you find they go well together. You'll find references in this book to that text. For example, instructions in an assignment might begin with "Refer to *PRW6e*, p. 321f, for some background on how to do this assignment." That is a suggestion to turn to page 321 and read it and the following pages for help before you tackle the assignment.

Learning to be a good public relations writer is learning to write with purpose. It isn't enough simply to master the mechanics of grammar, spelling and punctuation. They rank with learning to touch-type so you can produce prose on a typewriter or a word processor. Although these skills are important, they're technical skills. They deal only with the form of your writing, not its substance.

It has been traditional that public relations writers have a good many backups to review and edit their copy before it is used. That tradition has been weakened a lot in the last few years because of computers and other electronic aids. If you make a mistake of any kind now, it is more likely to be seen by people who shouldn't see it simply because there aren't as many sets of eyes—none, sometimes—reviewing what and how you write. That makes it all the more important that you learn to write correctly all the time. Writing it right is no longer a trite expression but an absolute requirement.

The goal of every piece of public relations writing is to get others to think or do something you want them to think or do. Such a task calls for high levels of preparation and strategic and creative thinking before you ever write a line. You must concentrate on six simple rules:

1. Understand your audience thoroughly.
2. Identify what is relevant to your audience, and why.
3. Match the message you want to send to the needs of your audience as your audience sees them, not as you perceive them.
4. Write a message acceptable to your audience.
5. Send your message through media to which your audience pays attention.
6. Deliver the message at the right time and as often as necessary to get it across.

If you always observe these six rules, your chances of becoming an effective public relations writer improve eventually. We add that qualifier because we don't know how serious you really are about think-time.

Think-Time

Think-time is the time you spend digging for information, analyzing and conceptualizing it and asking all sorts of "What if?" questions. It also includes the time you spend in rewriting a message until you write it right. Really successful writers spend most of their time as think-time.

Effective think-time requires self-discipline. Look at those six rules again. Only number four deals with the act of writing. The rest are concerned with thinking, analyzing, preparing to write and making decisions about to whom, when, how and how often messages will be delivered. Many beginning public relations writers ignore or forget those other five rules. They simply want to get on with the writing task. "I'm getting paid to write, not to be a researcher, planner or thinker. I just want to write."

We applaud the compulsion to fill blank pages. But we must ask, with what? Effective public relations writers deal with substance first and form second. It is simply an issue of priorities. Only when you are willing to prepare for writing will your wordsmithing skills pay off. The preparation we're talking about will be boring sometimes. But think-time can produce exciting results if you use it well. These ideas have led us to organize and structure this exercise book as we have.

Organization and Structure

All exercises and situations in this book happen in Serene, a fictional community in Serendipity County, USA. Read and study the information about Serene. Refer to it as often as necessary when you work with the exercises. If you wish, substitute your community for Serene, but please keep the organizations, issues, problems and situations in the exercises intact—as though they are happening in your community.

The Quick-Study pages preceding each new set of exercises are digests of information you should review thoroughly before trying the exercises. These digests summarize principles, points and issues drawn from chapters in the sixth edition of *Public Relations Writing: Form & Style*. Refer to that book for more detailed information.

Three scenarios are described before you get into the first set of exercises. Each scenario presents basic information you must refer to regularly, depending on which exercises you choose or which ones are assigned. Later exercises present new information and situations you must integrate into the context of the ongoing scenario. Working through the assignments related to a scenario teaches you how to put your writing skills into a context. Learning to use good techniques is one goal of this book. But an equally important goal is to help you to practice the art of synthesizing information and organizing it into a cohesive whole so that it communicates forcefully and is faithful to its purpose. Look at Martin Wank's complaints in Example 6:1.

The scenarios are fictional, but they are real in the sense that they are built around existing sources and similar situations. They represent an amalgamation of information and issues that we hope you find challenging and fun.

We urge you to work through the exercises related to one scenario. A scenario leads you through a broad range of writing tasks. And when you finish, you'll have a well-coordinated package of written materials that clearly shows how you can adapt your writing skills from one situation to another. You'll have a portfolio, "clips" if you will, that may make a good impression on potential employers.

If you prefer to work with independent assignments, you'll find them in each section. These exercises are effective when you're trying to learn the art of writing itself. But we're convinced you'll learn more about the central role good writing plays in public relations if you do the exercises related to a particular scenario.

You'll also find that think-time governs most of your success as a writer. Use your think-time wisely and you'll write with confidence and skill. Occasionally, you'll have to go to the library or consult the World Wide Web to get the information you need to handle some assignments with finesse.

In summary, then:

1. Research your subject and your audience.
2. Keep your audience and the medium in mind as you write.
3. Rewrite and polish.
4. Hone your language tools.
5. Lay your writing bare, down to the bone.

Special Thanks

Books are rarely the works only of the people named on title pages. That certainly is true of this book. We owe debts of thanks to many people for their help and inspiration. Among them are Karen Austin, editor, and Ryan Vesely, assistant editor, at Wadsworth Publishing Company, a division of International Thomson Publishing, Inc., Belmont, California. We also salute Rhett K. Fredric, M.D., P.A., a physician and friend in Fort Worth, Texas, for his insightful counsel regarding molecular biology. We also thank all the students who served as willing "guinea pigs" as we refined some of the assignments. Their insights and comments were invaluable.

Bob Carrell and Doug Newsom

Getting Started

P reparing to write is the critical first step in learning how to write
well. Writing well in public relations is learning to write with
careful attention given to a piece of writing's purpose and context.
Context is what this section on getting started is about. Study the material
below. It introduces you to fictional organizations, situations and people
who interact to form a fictional community. As you study them, try to
picture them clearly. Some are admirable. Others aren't. But many play
major or minor roles in some exercises you are about to do.

Serene, Serendipity County, U.S.A.

The last census counted Serene's population at 160,012, but Serendipity
County has a population of 212,112. Serene is also the county seat. Serene
provides goods and services for three counties with a combined population of 405,435. Because the main campus of State University also is located here, Serene is the commercial and educational hub of the south-
central part of the state. Although Serene has some light industrial manufacturers, its recent growth has been spurred mostly by high-tech research
and development firms and manufacturers attracted to an abundance of
electronic, scientific and business expertise available at the university.

Serene is connected to several metropolitan areas by north-south and east-
west interstate highways, although the nearest major market is 106 miles
away. The city is surrounded by rich agricultural land. Some mining goes
on, but it has declined sharply over the last 20 years. In 1960, 31 percent of
all jobs in the Serene area were related to mining; now that figure is only 2
percent. Amtrak provides regular rail service, and Peaceful Airport, 12
minutes north by car from downtown, provides nine round-trip flights

daily to two hub airports. Community leaders have had a difficult time, especially in the last 10 years, providing city services because Serenites have sometimes balked at appropriating new taxes and approving municipal bonds.

Mass Media and Agencies

Serene has a good selection of media for a market its size. The *Clarion* is an evening daily newspaper with Saturday morning and Sunday editions. Its format is full-size standard advertising unit (SAU). See Appendix A for an explanation of SAU. The *Clarion's* Sunday circulation averaged 89,323 last year, but the Monday to Saturday issues averaged 81,011. About 77 percent of the *Clarion's* circulation is within Serene city limits. It also offers a total market coverage (TMC) package. The living and food sections are wrapped in a four-page news section and mailed to every nonsubscriber household in the three-county trade territory for Thursday delivery.

The *Free Press* is a weekly newspaper with an average circulation of 8,689 last year. About 80 percent of its circulation is outside Serene city limits. Its strengths are its reports from rural correspondents, areawide school news and sports and coverage of the activities of county governments, especially road commissioners.

Radio Stations

Four radio stations originate signals in Serene. KICU-AM-FM is the State University station affiliated with National Public Radio (NPR). It takes most NPR feeds and originates some jazz and classical music programs. It also airs a one-hour rock music program daily at 10 P.M. that focuses on new artists, styles and albums. KICU news has won several reporting awards for aggressive pursuit of stories by student trainees. KARY-AM is a dawn-to-dusk operation that programs country-western music, but its news and sports are mostly rip-and-read. It does a superb job of reporting agricultural news, including markets and weather forecasts. KSKY-AM-FM is a 24-hour station that has a blend of light and easy listening music, interspersed with five-minute news segments, weather and sports on the hour. Its daily (no Sunday) 7 A.M. hour-long newscast is a wrap-up of overnight news locally and global news. Its daily (no Sunday) 30-minute noon newscast focuses on news from Washington, D.C., the state capital and Wall Street, including some brief market summaries. Its 6 P.M. hour-long newscast covers local, state, national and international news. As appropriate to the season, KSKY carries live intercollegiate sporting events in which State University teams compete. It is the most listened-to station by people 35 years or older. KISS-FM operates from 6 A.M. to midnight. Its programming is mostly rock, with some heavy metal thrown in. It does three rip-and-read, 15-minute newscasts daily, at 6 A.M., 11:45 A.M. and 6:45 P.M. It carries some talk shows that focus on music, musicians and other social icons.

Television Stations

Two television stations serve the area. One is the university-owned KICU-TV, Channel 13 (VHF), affiliated with the Public Broadcasting System (PBS). It does Monday to Friday, 30-minute magazine format newscasts that focus on university and Serene events and issues. The other television station is an independent, KWIK-TV, which broadcasts on Channel 25 (UHF). It does a 30-minute newscast at 7 A.M., noon, 6 P.M. and 10 P.M. Each consists of about 13 minutes of news and features, five minutes of weather and seven minutes of sports. Three 30-minute talk shows on Sunday depend on callers to question guests. One show focuses on city government and schools, another on economics and politics and the third on social services and issues.

A subsidiary of KWIK-TV is the local cable outlet, Kwik Cable Company (KCC), which imports and redistributes signals from 18 other sources, including ABC, CBS, NBC, ESPN, CNN, TNT, FOX, Showtime (SHOW), Cinemax (MAX), Disney and Arts and Entertainment (A&E). Additionally, KCC provides a public access channel (Channel 34, UHF) on which city council and school board meetings and the like are aired regularly. Serene's two public high schools also are hooked into the cable company. The schools provide some programs (most are taped) created with equipment supplied by KCC.

Public Relations and Advertising Agencies

Three agencies are located in Serene. One is Ideas, Inc., started four years ago by B.G. Deas. Ideas, Inc., employs a combination writer-designer and a secretary. It has made unsuccessful pitches to some regional advertising and public relations accounts, but the agency seems to survive, but barely, on local advertising accounts and an occasional public relations job. Clever Words, Inc., is another agency that seems to focus on accounts that need publicity and on special events. Cleve R. Word edited the local weekly for 10 years before he founded the agency in 1988. Most of Word's accounts are local, but the agency has done some regional promotions and special events during the last five years. The agency has six employees. Word is the president. Clever Words has two account executives: one an excellent writer, the other a talented designer and a production artist. There are two junior writers, neither of whom seems to be inspired, and a secretary.

Professional Communication Corporation

Professional Communication Corporation (ProCom) has operated in Serene for the last dozen years. It is owned and headed by I.M. Professor. She or he is your professor, who may prefer to be called by her or his proper name. She or he is dedicated to providing ProCom clients with the best service possible.

Although ProCom has just 20 employees, including Professor as president, the agency has a successful track record. It not only serves the Serene business community, but it also has several regional accounts and four national accounts. It is affiliated with a network of agencies in some major markets around the country. A client could hardly want a service that ProCom can't provide in-house or through an affiliate.

Professor is good at developing new accounts, especially with the support of Kari M. Backe who serves as executive vice president and account services supervisor. She has 20 years of account service work to her credit, having worked for major agencies in Los Angeles, Seattle, Chicago, Kansas City and New York City before joining ProCom eight years ago. Benjamin A. Counter has been vice president of finance and operations for two years. Professor hired him two years ago. Counter managed a plumbing supply house for six years before joining ProCom.

ProCom's Writers

ProCom also employs five account executives, four writers (three of whom are junior writers—*you are one of them*), two designers, a production artist, a broadcast and audiovisual specialist and four secretaries. Professor says ProCom soon will add two positions, director of research and senior writer.

Professor is regarded highly in many large-market agencies, and they find some of their best creative talent at ProCom. Professor often complains that ProCom is a training ground for the success of others, but Professor has such a commitment to helping young people start careers that these complaints are really expressions of pride.

Serene Chamber of Commerce

The Serene Chamber of Commerce has won several state and some national awards because of a very active membership. Although he is a longtime member of the Chamber, Richard R. Wilde, vice president for operations at Tentative Electronics, Inc., has been Chamber president just two months.

The first vice president is Glennis A. Klose. She is chief legal counsel at State University. Second vice president is Harry H. Usury, president of First American Bank. The Chamber's treasurer is Elliot T. Kincaid, owner and operator of The Serene Palace, a local nightspot that draws its customers mostly from the State University campus. The Chamber executive secretary is Ima H. Worker. She's held this spot 13 years.

The chairs of three major committees are Heddon T. Clouds, Economic Development Committee, A.W. Happy, Special Events Committee, and Justin J. Joiner, Membership Committee.

Serene City Council

The City Council has six ward seats from which the mayor is elected by council members present and voting. The mayor's term is two years. Ward terms are for three years, and are staggered so that two incumbents face reelection every year. Chairing the council for his third consecutive term is Darien W. Dorsey, who's in the first year of his fourth term representing Ward 6. Dorsey owns and operates the Serene Lincoln, Mercury and Ford dealership, a family business he inherited 15 years ago. Before that he served six years as sales director of a clothing manufacturer on the East Coast.

Purl E. Maye, who represents Ward 1, is a homemaker. She's devoted much of her time to volunteer service at the Serene Regional Hospital and to United Way. She headed the UW drive last year and exceeded its goal by 11 percent. She also sits on the board of directors of a major diversified energy company, Envire, Inc., whose subsidiaries include oil and gas exploration, pipeline operations, a state utility, and processing and distribution divisions. She's fond of saying that she was invited onto the board "as a token because I'm black, but not beautiful. I was quick to say yes, baby, because somebody's got to keep those honkies honest. It might as well be me." She gets things done. Perhaps that's why she's in her fourth term on the council.

Kary M. Backus represents Ward 2 and is in his first term. He owns and operates KARY-AM radio. He came to Serene eight years ago from the West Coast, where he was sales manager for a major line of heating and air-conditioning duct materials and supplies.

William (Bill) Belcher is in his second term from Ward 3. Belcher is Serene's leading restaurateur. He operates Strawberry Lake, noted for its nouvelle cuisine, and he has managers to run Pig Out, famous for its babyback ribs, and Abbaraccio (meaning "to embrace"), known for its northern Italian dishes. Belcher also owns 49 percent of three McDonald's franchises in Serene.

Tulley Howard Ho (his close friends call him Tally Ho) is a first-generation Vietnamese-American whose passion is agriculture and horses. He has accumulated several hundred acres around Serene where he has farming and horse operations (mostly thoroughbreds, but some quarter horses). He represents Ward 4. Because of the bloodlines, Ho's horse auctions draw major breeders and buyers from across the nation. He is in his second term on the council.

Robert N. Robbins, Ward 5, spends his full time managing his diversified investments portfolio, although he does consent to some financial consulting now and then. He inherited much of his holdings from his grandfather, who owned the Serene First Federal Savings and Loan for 42 years. The grandfather committed suicide when SFFS&L became insolvent four years ago. Robbins is in his first term on the council. As he's only 29, some council members disregard his opinions.

Serene School Board

The Serene school board has six members. They serve three-year staggered terms. The president is elected for a one-year term by board members present and voting. The board supervises two public high schools (grades 11 and 12), four junior high schools (grades 9 and 10), eight middle schools (grades 7 and 8) and 20 elementary schools (kindergarten through grade 6). The board in recent years has been sharply divided on issues of school size, financing and operating policies. However, these conflicts are smoothed over, so the board seems harmonious to the public.

Oscar T. House is in his third term on the board, but it is his second as president. He is chairman of the board of directors of Tentative Electronics, Inc. (TEI), a small but growing manufacturer of electronics equipment and supplies used in the financial community nationwide. Its over-the-counter stock uses the NASDAQ symbol TEI and closed yesterday at $2 per share. Ector Z. Million is in his fourth term as a school board member. He is vice president of operations at the Serene National Bank.

Pauline B. Pundus is in the second year of her first term. She is currently president of the local chapter of the Daughters of the American Revolution (DAR). Ms. Pundus's family settled in the Serene area more than 150 years ago. She earned her doctorate in American Studies at the University of Minnesota, but her other degrees in humanities are from the State University in Serene. Her fiancé was killed in an automobile accident 28 years ago, 48 hours before their wedding day, and she has never married. At 52, she lives alone on the family estate with her dog, Blossom, a frisky Boston Terrier. Pundus Avenue is one of Serene's main downtown streets, and Pundus Park, southwest of central Serene, is named for her father.

Esther Little-Deere is an attorney married to Marcus F. Deere, also an attorney. She runs the staff of the public defender's office. She's in her first term on the board. Persistent rumors claim she wants to be district attorney so that she can use that job as a stepping stone to a statewide post. Robert N. Jester owns and operates the Serene Comedy Club and Bar. He is not taken seriously by other board members, even though he's in his third term. Alan A. Sellers is the advertising director of KWIK-TV. He's in the first year of his first term on the board. He's generally regarded as a "young man to watch" because of his brains, drive and persistence.

State University at Serene

State University at Serene (SUS) is one of 12 state university campuses. It has a board of regents that reports to the State Higher Education Board that sets budget allocations and overall operating and curricular policies for the state-wide system. SUS is noted for the strength of its teaching and research faculty in the hard sciences and business, although it also has strong programs in the social sciences and the arts. Its School of Law is small, but it is generally regarded as the best in the state.

Dr. Thomas S. Lott, 48, is president of SUS, a post he's held the last five years. Dr. Lott came to SUS from the presidency of a small liberal arts college in Ohio. He holds the bachelor of science in biology from the University of Tennessee, the master of science in molecular biology from the University of Illinois and the doctor of philosophy in genetics from Northwestern University. He has authored more than three dozen refereed articles in the leading journals of biology and has one of the leading principles texts in the field. He is regarded as a superb scientist and an able administrator, although some people believe he is not as politically astute as he should be.

During his first year as president, he hired Dr. Marie E. Westenberger as provost of SUS. As provost, Dr. Westenberger, now in her fourth year, acts as president when Dr. Lott is away from the campus. As provost, she has direct responsibility for the internal workings of the campus, leaving Dr. Lott free to concentrate on external affairs. Dr. Westenberger holds baccalaureate, master and doctor of philosophy degrees in sociology and psychology from the University of Chicago. The president chose Dr. Westenberger to complement his own lack of depth in the social sciences and the arts. Seven deans report to the provost. They are: Dr. Joel P. McNally, dean of the School of Sciences, Dr. Ellen H. Jacoby, dean of the School of Social Sciences, Dr. Robert L. Lewellyn, dean of the School of Law, Dr. Shirley M. Kelley, dean of the School of Fine Arts, Dr. Terrell H. Thompson, dean of the School of Engineering, Dr. Mallory M. Malcom, dean of the School of Medicine and Dr. Gerald L. Sweedlow, dean of the School of Business. Edgar M. Burns, director of student financial aid, also reports directly to Dr. Westenberger.

Yancy S. Mann, director of information services, and Nathaniel B. Isaccs, director of financial and auxiliary services (such as dormitories, cafeterias, maintenance, grounds, etc.), report to Dr. Lott, as does Andrew W. Cooper, director of development.

Enrollment at SUS in the current term is 22,239 of which 2,102 are graduate students, including 304 in doctoral programs, three fourths of whom are in the sciences. SUS limits enrollment of undergraduates to those who finish high school in the top 10 per cent of their classes and have ACT or SAT scores at least 50 per cent better than the national average. Graduate students are screened by a rigid set of criteria so that only about one in twenty applicants gets admitted. Bio-chemistry and molecular biology are the two programs in most demand because of the outstanding faculty in these areas. A Cray super computer, one of the largest and fastest in the world, is a principal research tool that attracts both new faculty and students.

The cost of graduate programs at SUS is about 20 per cent higher than on the other 11 state university campuses. This fact is a bone of contention among these campuses because their leaders often claim preferential budget treatment by the State Higher Education Board. SUS has been successful over several decades, of course, in getting increased state funding and has built its programs in the sciences to world-class status. But state funding has also been helped by an extensive program of funded research and a generous endowment of nearly one billion dollars, much of it earmarked for support of teaching and research in the sciences.

Serene Politicians

U.S. Sen. Herchel H. Hanzout lives in Serene. Although some say he's not well liked by his constituents, he has beaten all challengers and has been in Washington 14 years. He now chairs the powerful Ways and Means Committee. The family has been in politics for decades, although Herchel is the first Hanzout to serve in Washington. His father served two terms as governor, and his grandfather was speaker of the State House of Representatives for 22 years. Hanzout earned his baccalaureate degree (B.A.) in political science from Princeton and has a Master of Business Administration degree (M.B.A.) from Harvard. He was a third-year law student when he quit to make his first Senate race. Hanzout's wife, Paula, is a sister to Pauline Pundus. Mrs. Hanzout was educated at Vassar and studied art for three years at the Sorbonne. They have three children, two of whom are married and live out of state. The youngest attends State University. She is a fifth-year senior with a double major in public relations and classics and minors in computer science and statistics.

State Rep. P.N. Barrell also lives in Serene and is in his sixth term. He represents Serendipity County and a small section of an adjoining county. He serves on several important committees, but, according to him, he's declined chairing any of them because he prefers to work "behind the scenes." He has cosponsored several controversial bills, some of which became law, but he's never authored a bill himself. He worked his way through college and law school.

He has made a name for himself as a tough defense attorney, who has successfully defended people in several celebrated criminal cases. Although he's only 48, he's amassed in the last 15 years an estate whose estimated worth is more than $20 million. He dresses flamboyantly and has married and divorced three times. His marriages have produced no offspring, but he's rumored to be the father of two, a boy 11 and a girl 6, each with a different mother.

Notes

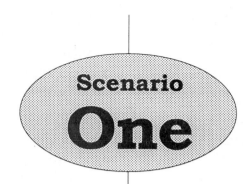

GenEcon, Inc.

GenEcon, Inc. (GEI) is a start-up. It began November 1 last year with an infusion of $10 millions in venture capital from Omega Venture Capital of Chicago. Omega is a consortium of investors who believe that the 21st century will become known as the biotech age. As a biotech organization, GenEcon's purpose is to do basic research into the relationship between genes and disease. The hope is that GenEcon research will help fill some of the voids in the genetic maps of all living organisms, especially humans. A commercial laboratory has announced that it has completed the human genome, but some scientists are skeptical. As these voids are filled, the chances of developing effective cures and preventive treatments for a range of human diseases may increase dramatically. This new information may also add significantly to our ability to eliminate or control more effectively some plant and animal diseases, thus increasing productivity.

Primer on Genes and DNA

The blueprint of life is DNA (deoxyribonucleic acid). DNA is a long, double helix chain built by linking four simple molecules known as *adenine, quanine, thymine* and *cytosine*. The order in which they are linked determines the kind of genetic information each chain contains. It is this *sequence* of molecules that scientists are trying to decode. All of the DNA in an organism is known as the *genome*. Genes have hundreds or thousands of simple molecules. Each gene holds the genetic instructions to make another type of crucial molecule—*protein*. Proteins include everything from hormones such as insulin that regulates blood-sugar levels to enzymes that help digest food. Some proteins turn on or off other genes that can affect other genes, thus forming feedback loops.

Proteins are characterized as tiny but important cogs in complex biological systems. For example, thousands of genes and proteins work together in the human immune system to control an army of cells and *antibodies*—another type of protein—against invaders. When they don't work harmoniously, people get sick.

The DNA in each cell of the human body contains all the information needed to produce a person. At any given moment, some genes are active while others are dormant. That explains why a skin cell is different from a kidney cell. Different sets of genes are turned on or off in each.

Scientists are perplexed at understanding how the 80,000 or so genes in a human turn themselves on and off in combinations that produce a human being. But they have made progress in discovering and describing quite a range of genes and proteins that have begun to fill out *biological pathways*. For example, one pathway is the process by which cells turn glucose into enough energy for a person to run a marathon.

Genes can go haywire. A "misspelling" in just one letter—resulting in an improper or missing link in a DNA chain—is called a *mutation*. A change in a single link of the thousands in a gene can cause diseases, such as anemia. More complex illnesses—such as heart disease and cancer—may be caused not just by a single mutation but by a combination.

Genetic researchers aim to find these faulty genes and to figure out why their biological pathways get fouled up. Mapping the human genome is like creating a *genetic map*. This is something like a genetic atlas that shows the locations of genes that have been mapped successfully. Each of these is called a *marker*—something of a signpost—which may be used to identify genes that might relate to diseases. It is easier to find Bartlesville, OK if you know that it's just north of Tulsa. If you want to find a certain gene, it also is easier if you know that it is near a certain marker. This process is illustrated by researchers who seek markers among members of families afflicted with inherited diseases. When the markers are located, they know that affected genes are nearby and thus can focus their research efforts more narrowly.

Finding and mapping genes is time-consuming, costly and frustrating. Because there are so many voids in the genomes of so many organisms, researchers have shunned a scattershot approach in favor of trying to sequence entire genomes, link by link. It is expected that thousands of new genes will be found, as well as extra genetic information that may be found between genes. As new information is added, the door to understanding the basis of life is opened ever wider.

The Biotech Future

The 20th century was transformed by the computer chip. The 21st century may well be transformed by the development of more and more genomes that map the genetic make-up of living organisms. A few genomes have already been completed. Scientists are busy working on filling in the gaps in hundreds of others. As the number of completed genomes increases, they are expected to do for biological research what the periodic table of elements did for chemistry in the 20th century.

There is a long, well-known history of crude attempts at genetic engineering. Hybridizing of plants has led to more disease-resistant and improved plants that produce more productive crops. Selective breeding of domestic animals has also produced improved, even new, bloodlines in livestock.

What the current work in biotechnology will lead to is open to speculation. But there are some indications. For example, the bacterium *hemophilus* was the first genome to be fully mapped. This bacterium is known to cause meningitis and ear infections in children. Researchers are using this knowledge as a springboard to develop new drugs and vaccines. Other scientists are working furiously along several avenues of attack. For example, Motorola is working on gene splicing and genome engineering in which researchers hope to use a DNA model as the basis for the design of a new type of computer vastly more powerful and faster than traditional digital systems. In fact, primitive DNA computers have already been developed by a few university faculties. It may be that new information from research on the mustard weed, for example, will let farmers grow plants with enough plastic to reduce our dependency on fossil fuels.

These and many similar developments are exciting to scientists who now can think of problems on a grander scale. They now seek and expect to get answers to questions they didn't know to ask in the not-to-distant past. Many of them fully expect to know everything that goes into the make-up of a living cell in the not-to-distant future. It is this glimpse of the future that inspired the formation of GenEcon, Inc.

The Dolly Factor

A little-known Scottish embryologist, Ian Wilmut, shocked the world when he announced that he and his team of researchers at Roslin Institute—just outside Edinburgh—had cloned a sheep they named Dolly. Dolly was created by taking the DNA from the mammary gland of a sheep and inserting it into the womb of another Dorset sheep. The DNA from the lamb turned out to be an exact copy, or clone. The name Dolly presumably was selected in recognition of the mammary glands of Dolly Parton. Wilmut contends that the same principle should work with any mammal—including humans.

Cloning domestic animals or plants is not far removed from plant hybridizing or selective breeding. But cloning humans may be another matter. In the first place, it may not be possible because some genetic experiments show that what works in mice does not work in rats, and vice versa. This suggests that all mammals are not the same. Certainly, humans are more complex.

If further experiments show that Dolly isn't a fluke, the dramatic consequences for farm and ranch production are only a beginning. Should cloning of people be both possible and practical, think of the dazzling but equally troublesome possibilities. The parents of a dying child might consider cloning the child. Some people might want to clone themselves as a way of gaining a measure of immortality. In the hands of some people like Adolph Hitler who aspired to the development of a superior race, the cloning of humans raises an enormous range of political, legal and ethical questions. Should physicians test for genetic conditions they can do nothing about? If so, would employers and insurance companies be privy to the results? Some people believe that we aren't yet prepared to address questions and issues like these and similar ones nor, perhaps, are we willing to implement their solutions.

Questions and issues like these are generally far removed from the forefront of concern of scientists who are focused on unraveling the mysteries of DNA. They are driven more by the desire to know and the exhilaration of discovery than they are by political, legal or ethical issues. But Dolly has cloaked genetic experiments with a sense of widespread urgency rarely seen in the scientific community. To say that Dolly has inspired an enormous interest in molecular biology, not just among scientists but by a broad range of people around the world, is a gross understatement.

Post-Dolly Developments: Bar-Coded Bodies

The Dolly phenomenon opened a new vista on the possibilities for the development of disease resistant, more productive plants and animals and new techniques for diagnosing human ailments and their treatment or prevention. Scientific work at mapping the human genome continues at a rapid pace, but public attention seems to be on the cloning process, fed especially by comments by a maverick scientist who says he could clone humans now. He hasn't, of course. Even if humans could be cloned, a nagging question is whether they should be. Nevertheless, successful cloning experiments of cows, pigs and other animals have followed closely on the heels of the Dolly announcement.

The term cloning can be confusing. Scientists use it in two primary ways. One is *reproductive* cloning, *i.e.*, creating an entire animal from a single cell by asexual reproduction. The other is *therapeutic* cloning in which cloning technology is used to create organ replacements or skin tissue that won't be rejected by recipients. Single-cell organisms, such as bacteria and fungi, have been cloned in research laboratories for decades. Their products are used in fermentation processes such as in bread or beer production. Taking cuttings from plants—a practice for centuries—can also be described as cloning because it involves creating an entire plant from a small number of cells by asexual reproduction.

There's also *transgenic manipulation,* a process in which genes from one specie are implanted in a different specie. This is an old technique relative to plants but it is new to mammals. Researchers are also experimenting with transgenic processes for use in growing organs that could be transplanted to humans with reduced risk of rejection. A ready supply of replacement hearts, livers, lungs, kidneys and other organs is a heady goal, giving credence to what one wag has called bar-coded bodies.

One of the most provocative ideas to emerge recently is the intent to implant DNA from a wooly mammoth in an Asian female elephant. A whole wooly mammoth—which lived about 23,00 years ago—has been excavated from an ice field in Siberia and is currently being kept frozen while a team of internatonal scientists study it. Skeptics say the odds for success are very slim because the DNA from the mammoth is so old and may be too damaged for use. However, university researchers have produced a cow from the DNA of another that had been dead for more than a year.

The eruption of genetic information is not only transforming the practice of medicine but also the way crimes are solved. England in 1995 began a national DNA data base. The United States is preparing one. Forensic scientists routinely use DNA evidence in their attempts to identify badly mutilated bodies in plane crashes, for example, or decomposed bodies at sites of massacres, as in Kosovo. And it is becoming common to use DNA testing to establish paternity.

GenEcon's Game Plan

The work of GenEcon is not a game, but a serious quest to answer perplexing questions about molecular structures that may lead to copyrights, patents or licenses, each of which may produce enormous economic rewards. The organization is structured to conduct research on molecular structures in plants, domestic animals and humans. It is not expected that accomplishments by GenEcon scientists will be distributed equally among all three broad areas. In fact, it is anticipated that discoveries, even by accident, may eventually lead management to put more resources in one area than in others, even to the extent that some research venues may be abandoned. Scientists working in a program area designated to be phased out will have the option to shift to another area, if appropriate. If not, scientists with appropriate credentials will be sought as replacements.

This basic strategy led GenEcon's founders to recruit a wide range of talent, but focused on molecular biologists and cytogenetists. With the infusion of venture capital from Omega, management recruited an initial pool of 21 scientists and a support staff of 36. Although there is sufficient venture capital to launch its research programs, GenEcon expects each of its scientists to begin generating funding within two years from government and private foundation grants sufficient to cover salaries, benefits and basic research expenses. That expectation was part of the initial employment agreement with all new recruits. It also made it necessary for GenEcon to focus on scientists with extensive experience at grantsmanship, in addition to their research successes.

The decision to locate in Serene was influenced primarily by the concentration of highly qualified group of biochemists and molecular biologists at the State University. Negotiations with the university administration and academic leaders led GenEcon to believe that its private research operations would find invaluable scientific counsel nearby. Also, the university's administration agreed to lease time on its Cray super computer at a very favorable rate. In exchange for this favorable treatment, GenEcon agreed that its scientists would be available for cooperative research with university faculty. Access to a Cray and the proximity of a group of respected colleagues was seen as a plus by many of the scientists who accepted GenEcon's offer.

GenEcon leased a large building adjacent to the University's campus. The building needed only nominal modifications—which the property owner provided— to convert it into a state-of-the art research facility. There also is sufficient space to allow for doubling of the building's size if that becomes necessary. Although GenEcon bought some new laboratory equipment, it leases most of its sophisticated equipment, so capital investment was kept low. This was a necessary strategy to allow GenEcon to recruit the scientists and support staff it wanted.

GenEcon Principals

Glen E. E. Kowan, 45, is the chairman of the board and chief executive officer of GenEcon. Kowan was a chief scientist at the Institute for Genetic Research for 11 years before resigning to form his own company. Kowan's credentials include a Bachelor of Science in Biochemistry from the University of Chicago, the Master of Science in genetics from the California Institute of Technology and the Doctor of Philosophy in embryology from the University of Michigan. He has done post-doctoral study in molecular biology under the auspices of the National Science Foundation at the University of Texas at Austin. Prior to joining IGR, Kowan was on the faculty of the Department of Biology at the University of Kansas for eight years where he distinguished himself for his molecular experiments. Friends and colleagues often describe Kowan as a visionary whose creativity often sparkles with genius but they also say that administrative and bureaucratic details drive him to distraction.

Kowan was well liked and respected by his colleagues at both Kansas and IGR. He also was rewarded well economically at both places but he longed for the freedom to be his own boss so he could pursue research of his own choosing and to benefit from its success. That prompted him to develop the idea that led to GenEcon.

While at IGR, Kowan became close personally and professionally with Lowell U. Garrett, LUG to his friends. In time it became clear to Kowan that Garrett had similar needs. So they talked about them for more than three years before resigning to set up GenEcon. The plan was for Garrett to be the executive vice president whose primary responsibility was to coordinate all of the research efforts implemented by GenEcon scientists. Unlike Kowan, Garrett, 39, seems to have a keen talent for organization and following through on details. Garrett's Doctor of Philosophy in cyto-genetics is from Texas A. and M. University. His Bachelor of Science in genetics is from Louisiana State University and his Master of Science in biochemistry is from the University of Kentucky. He was on the biology faculty at the University of Georgia eight years before joining Kowan at IGR where they later became friends.

Two other people complete the management team of GenEcon. Amanda Etherly is vice president for finance and administration and Evelyn Drewhurst is vice president for corporate communication. Etherly, 37, has a Bachelor of Business Administration in management form New York

University and the Master of Business Administration in finance from Syracuse. She worked six years as an actuarian for State Farm Insurance and the last nine years as director of purchasing for the manufacturer of Mack trucks. Colleagues say she has a clear, sharp mind that reduces most ideas and concepts to numbers and is especially gifted at developing and implementing cost control systems.

Drewhurst, 34, joined GenEcon after eight years as an account executive with Burson-Marstellar in Chicago. Before that she worked three years in the corporate communication offices of the Ford Motor Company, first as a writer and then as special events coordinator. Her Bachelor of Arts in political science is from the University of Tennessee and her Master of Arts in communication is from the University of Florida. She seems to be accepted as a valuable member of the management team and is consulted about the communication implications of all policy decisions. Her advice is usually followed, but she sometimes has trouble working closely with Kowan whose attention span is limited because he is so focused on GenEcon's primary mission—genetic research.

The management team meets each Monday at 10 A.M., expecting to adjourn no later than noon. Other meetings are called now and then. It is routine that Kowan sets the agenda and guides the conversation and decisions. Decisions are usually arrived at amicably but Kowan sometimes finds himself in opposition to the other three. When this happens, weekly or called meetings may run well beyond the noon hour. Compromise with Kowan is sometimes quite hard to achieve.

Relations with Omega Venture Capital

Two of the principal investors at Omega Venture Capital are long-time friends of Kowan. That's why Kowan went to Omega as a source of funding. Wiliam D. Gunther who grew up on a small farm in southern Nebraska met Kowan at the University of Chicago where they struck a lasting friendship. Gunther's field of study was finance, not science. He went into training with a brokerage house after graduation. After 12 years of making prudent personal investments, he left the firm to focus entirely on the management of his own portfolio, now estimated to be worth about $150 millions.

While he was still with the brokerage, Gunther also developed a lasting friendship with Donald R. Buchendorf, one of his clients. Gunther's advice helped Buchendorf turn a modest investment into a portfolio of more than $90 millions in less than 10 years. When Kowan was in Chicago on business several years ago, he called Gunther to set up a dinner date.

When Gunther met Kowan, he had Buchendorf in tow. Kowan and Gunther liked each other immediately.

It was only natural that Kowan would turn to Gunther and Buchendorf regarding venture capital. Negotiating the investment proved relatively easy to complete, including the full support of the other four principals at Omega. The initial agreement was for $10 millions, but with the understanding that up to another $20 millions might be needed before income from grants would exceed operating expenses. The contract between GenEcon and Omega specifies that the two firms will share equally in the net profits from copyrights, patents and licenses and that Gunther and Buchendorf will sit on GenEcon's advisory board.

Advisory Board

As its name implies, the board evaluates and advises GenEcon's management team on research issues and policies. Kowan presides at advisory board meeting, but all of the management team is present and participates in presentations and discussions. A primary concern of the advisory board is to keep the management team fully briefed on contemporary activities in the sciences, especially in molecular biology. Advisory board members also are expected to be sounding boards and reflections of opinions on public policy issues. Issues surrounding the idea of cloning are especially vital because of the work at GenEcon.

The board has 12 members who meet quarterly. Harold W. Wright, Ph.D., is professor of life sciences at the University of Chicago. Arnold S. Ziffern, Ph.D., is professor of biochemistry and a Nobel winner at the University of North Carolina. Alonzo Bernardi, Ph.D., is professor of embryology at Syracuse University. Maxwell M. Meadows, Ph.D., is professor of biology and a Nobel winner at the University of Illinois, Urbana. William F. Cotton, Ph.D., is professor of biochemistry at University of Southern California. Roberta A. Flesch, Ph.D., is professor of plant pathology at Arizona State University. Two others are physicians. One is a cardiologist, Hubert N. Massengill, M.D., in Dallas. The other is an oncologist, Fallis A. Smythe, M.D., in Kansas City. The final two seats are held by Clarence D. Summers of Louisville, Kentucky, president and CEO of Fisher Banks, a chain of banks in the southeastern states, and Glen G. Davis of Denver, president and CEO of Earth Harvest Foods, a major food processing and marketing firm.

Notes

National Association of Trauma Specialists

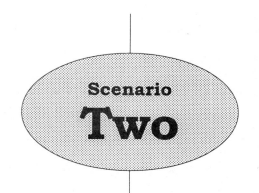

Scenario **Two**

The National Association of Trauma Specialists (NATS) was organized in 1956 in Chicago by doctors specializing in emergency medicine. It is an association of practicing and retired physicians who elected to specialize in the study and treatment of trauma as the primary cause of deaths among people injured in accidents.

History

Studies of casualty statistics from World War II suggested that about 65 percent of the deaths from battlefield wounds resulted more from the trauma induced by the wounds than from the wounds themselves. Trauma can be described generally as a shock to the human body induced by any external agent. That statistic led medical researchers to theorize that rapid treatment to stabilize traumatized soldiers would increase time for effective treatment of the wounds themselves.

The theory was put into practice during the Korean War (although some people still prefer to call that war a police action). Mobile Army Surgical Hospitals (M.A.S.H., as in the movie and television series of the same name) were set up close to the front lines. Helicopters carried the wounded quickly to these field hospitals. Although some repair and treatment of wounds was done by M.A.S.H. units, their primary purpose was to treat the trauma and stabilize wounded soldiers as quickly as possible. The wounded were then taken to more fully equipped hospitals for appropriate treatment, surgical reconstruction or other therapeutic procedures.

The concept proved so successful in reducing battlefield deaths that after the war some surgeons adapted the method to civilian practice. It wasn't long before medical students began preparing for careers in the practice of emergency medicine. This produced a small stream of new physicians especially trained to treat major injuries, such as those that occur in automobile accidents. Each year a staggering number of deaths is caused by accidents in the United States. The practice of emergency medicine has mushroomed.

The Association

More than 12,000 physicians and other medical personnel were members of NATS at the end of last year. They are mostly from the United States, but 18 percent of them are from 22 foreign countries. Because of the high cost of equipping and staffing a complete trauma treatment unit, most emergency rooms staffed with trauma specialists are found only in larger hospitals (about 18 percent of the total).

Doctors specializing in emergency medicine must complete a specialty residency following completion of their medical studies. The association offers continuing education programs to doctors and other personnel. These programs are often presented at various medical schools or teaching hospitals, with sessions usually lasting from two to five days each. The annual NATS convention also offers technical training sessions as well as medical papers that explain the latest research findings in trauma diagnosis and treatment.

NATS Communication Program

The NATS communication program includes a monthly newsletter, *Traumatic*. It features research findings in brief, the association's lobbying efforts at the state and national levels and interpretations of and opinions about proposed legislation that might affect emergency care. Technical bulletins, known as *Traumatech*, are distributed periodically during the year to the membership. The number of bulletins has ranged annually from nine to 27 during the last five years. A quarterly four-color journal, *Emergency Medicine*, circulates not only to NATS members but also to other members of the American Medical Association (AMA) and hospital administrators. The editorial thrust emphasizes the positive aspects of emergency medicine and the need to expand facilities and staff.

NATS Problems

For two primary reasons, morale among NATS members is poor and falling.

First, emergency room physicians work a 70-hour week, on the average. This is not only physically demanding and debilitating, but it also takes them away from their families, resulting in higher divorce, alcohol and drug abuse rates than in any other segment of the medical community.

Second, the demand on most major emergency rooms is about 133 percent beyond planned capacity. Thus, if you walk through a major hospital emergency room, you'll probably find patients in hallways and lounges waiting for treatment because treatment rooms are full.

Membership Survey

A recent survey shows that 71.5 percent of the NATS membership sees the combination of hours and workload as untenable. An internal analysis of membership trends, completed last Tuesday, shows that the association, starting two years ago, began to lose 20 members for each 19 it gained. This analysis has not been reported to the association, although that is expected to happen soon, nor has it been shared with the public.

One of the most disturbing statistics related to emergency room medicine is that about 60 percent of those treated are involved in preventable accidents. About 30 percent of these preventable accidents are auto accidents involving alcohol or drug abuse.

Furthermore, about 25 percent of those who seek emergency treatment aren't emergencies at all. Stomachaches, headaches, sore muscles and non-emergency conditions like minor cuts should wait to be treated by the patients' own physicians.

Emergency Room Overload

The NATS leadership believes much of the emergency room overload is attributable to these non-emergency cases because the public is not educated enough about the legitimate uses and purposes of emergency room medicine. Cases abound where accident victims have died or nearly died unnecessarily because emergency room facilities were clogged by people seeking treatment for minor cuts, scrapes and diarrhea.

Another issue is that some people, because they can't afford to buy health insurance or to see a personal physician regularly, may turn to emergency rooms for their health care. The problem is that they tend to put off proper treatment because they can't afford it. As an illness worsens, it may result in a visit to an emergency room. For example, a staph infection in the throat usually can be treated inexpensively and easily if diagnosed early enough. An infection like that left alone can quickly become a major medical case. Treatment that could have been inexpensive is often the most expensive because the illness is worse and it requires much more intensive medical attention and treatment. This problem also may occur when a person's HMO refuses ER admission.

Serene and NATS

NATS was founded and headquartered in Chicago until seven years ago when it moved to Serene. The board of directors, in concert with the association's executive team, recommended to the membership, which approved it overwhelmingly by mail ballot, the move to Serene for five major reasons:

1. The State University has a large medical complex in Serene.
2. Two members of the university's acclaimed medical faculty won two consecutive Nobel Prizes in medicine. Both are emergency medicine specialists.
3. The state medical school is generally recognized as being on the leading edge of emergency room diagnosis and treatment, research and practices.
4. A good transportation system makes it easy for even international visitors, and there are many of them, to travel to and from Serene.
5. Serene is in a semi-pastoral setting that appeals to middle- and upper-income families, and there is no town-and-gown split in the community.

Major Players at NATS

The executive staff of NATS is headed by H. Arthur (Arty) Hart, who has served as executive director for 10 years. His medical degree and emergency room studies focused on thoracic medicine (the chest cavity). Barry

P. Tallant, director of operations, is not a physician but has an M.B.A. degree from State University in operations management. Many of the NATS staff see him as a buttoned-down, three-piece pinstriper who won't be at NATS much longer because his ambition is to run his own organization.

The director of financial affairs is Patricia (Patsy) R. Bills. She has advanced degrees in nursing and worked six years in a major hospital emergency room before joining NATS three years ago. She joined NATS so that she could use her certified public accountancy training to the benefit of the association.

The director of communication is Sally S. Forth, who came to NATS just two months ago. Her B.A. and M.A. degrees from State University are in public relations. She's spent the last three years as research director at a major agency in New York City. Before that she handled account services in Dallas and Atlanta for six years and was in creative services three years for a major firm in San Francisco. Ms. Forth has a staff of four, plus two interns from State University.

Board of Directors

The six members of the NATS board of directors are elected to two-year staggered terms by secret ballot at the annual convention by members present and voting. The board elects its own chair. Hart Z. Smart, M.D., from Kansas City, Mo., is the current chair. Other members are Harry O. Leggs, M.D., Lincoln, Neb.; Walter F. Armes, M.D., Corpus Christi, Tex.; Brooke N. Bonze, M.D., Syracuse, N.Y.; Turner R. Head, M.D., San Diego, Calif., and Tyre D. Blood, M.D., Denver, Colo. The immediate past president also sits on the board in an advisory capacity. She is Sterling S. Goodheart, M.D., Alexandria, Va.

Notes

National Child-Care Centers

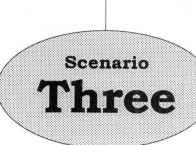

Scenario **Three**

National Child-Care Centers (NCCC) was founded in 1969 to provide quality day-care and child development programs to children from 2 to 12 years old. NCCC was founded by William (Will) Diaperchange and his wife, Needa. But in 1987 they sold NCCC to a holding company that has subsidiaries in the fields of nursing homes (geriatric care), institutional food processing and preparation, catering and others. The formal name of the holding company is Bottoms, Armes, Betters and Yema, Inc., but it goes by the acronym BABY. BABY is traded over the counter (NASDAQ symbol: BABI). The Diaperchanges no longer participate in the management of NCCC except as members of BABY's board of directors.

Beginning Philosophy

The Diaperchanges founded and operated NCCC on one guiding principle: to integrate educational and developmental training with traditional day-care services. Perhaps it is an unfair characterization, but at that time day-care centers were little more than holding pens for the children of working parents. Although toys abounded and some planned activities were included in most day-care operations, few centers even attempted to integrate childhood developmental programs into their operations. Three primary reasons account for this initially haphazard approach:

1. Center operators believed parents were unwilling or unable to pay the higher costs of such programs.

2. There was a shortage of properly trained personnel whom centers could hire at modest salaries.

3. Most physical facilities were inadequate to the demands of this educational approach.

Most people in the child-care business then thought that the falling birth-rate of the 1960s and 1970s signaled a declining market for day-care centers for years to come. They also thought existing private caregivers could easily absorb the number of children entering the day-care market. In general, operators concluded that the demand for full-scale child development and day-care centers was economically unsound and would not attract attention from major investors.

A Different Perspective

The Diaperchanges thought differently. They agreed that the market was only a small percentage of the total number of children needing daycare. But they also believed that children of the 1980s and 1990s, although a small percentage of the total population, would belong mostly to parents reared in the 1960s and 1970s, who, research suggested, valued the quality of life and the opportunities for advancement for their own children. Will and Needa saw these parents and their progeny as part and parcel of the "me generation," as these people were referred to by social commentators.

They further thought that enough of these parents not only would want more daycare for their children, but would look for caregivers whose skills would speed up their children's social and educational development. And they were willing and able to pay for it. Among other interpretations, the Diaperchanges also realized that centers with developmental goals must be conveniently located for these parents. They concluded that these parents probably would be willing to pay more for quality care, but they might be equally unwilling, because of time constraints, to make extended daily side trips to get it.

The Center Is Born

The first Child Care Center was opened in Dallas, Texas, in 1983. It was located on Stemmons Freeway because most forecasts indicated that the areas north and west of downtown Dallas were the most promising for future residential growth. Parents who commute via Stemmons could drop off or pick up their children quickly and easily, thus eliminating time-consuming side trips.

The center was designed with 10 activity rooms, each with a capacity of 10 children. It also included offices for staff, an emergency medical care room, a central assembly hall and a kitchen for preparing and serving hot, nutritious meals. A large portico let parents drive under cover to drop off or pick up their children during bad weather. The grounds were not spacious, but there was ample space for swings, jungle gyms, seesaws, sandboxes and the like.

Because neither Will nor Needa Diaperchange had such training, they hired a specialist in early childhood development. She was named director and was responsible for operating the center and its programs. Although all teachers at the center were not required to hold degrees, the policy was that each supervisor of every age level must have at least one degree and at least three years of professional experience in early childhood development.

Big Business and Child Care

These early decisions by the Diaperchanges were astute: The first center quickly filled to capacity. Soon the word *national* was added to form NCCC, and by 1988 the NCCC network included 55 centers in Texas, Oklahoma, Louisiana, Kansas and Missouri. By this time, an "echo boom" in the U.S. birthrate had occurred as the children of the so-called baby boom began to reach their 30s.

This "echo boom" resulted in an attractive market opportunity because upwardly mobile young professionals with substantial disposable incomes were at last producing children. Many of these were two-career families.

The child-care market at last had impressive demographics, and psychographics began to attract the interest of big investors looking for profitable opportunities. Several national chains were formed to compete with existing caregivers. Names such as Kindercare, La Petite Academy and Daybridge became prominent.

Enter BABY

BABY, with corporate headquarters in Chicago, became interested. The marketing department at BABY recommended that an existing daycare group be bought. BABY was first rebuffed by Daybridge and then by Kindercare before management decided to go to the founders of the market—NCCC and the Diaperchanges.

Because they had no children and only a few distant relatives with whom they were not close, Will and Needa had talked privately about the need for a succession plan or the possibility of a sale. They were also aware of their ages. Will was then 59 and Needa was 60. Both were in relatively good health.

Negotiators from BABY found willing ears at their first meeting with the Diaperchanges in late January 1989. After several meetings, a deal was struck March 1, 1989, in which $28 million in BABY stock was transferred to Will and Needa, and they became BABY board members for life. The NCCC name was to continue but as a subsidiary of BABY.

Under BABY's ownership, NCCC has grown rapidly and now includes 112 centers in 17 states, none in cities with a population of less than 150,000. The original concept of the center and its design have been retained. The only structural change has been, because of growth, to organize NCCC operations into districts with a maximum of 10 centers in each. Each district is headed by a supervisor who reports to NCCC corporate headquarters in Dallas.

The Program

The rate for developmental child care at an NCCC center is $175 weekly per child. Each child is assigned to a room with children of the same age and/or level of educational development.

Each room has at least one teacher with degree qualifications in childhood development and enough teacher aides, some of whom are working on degree programs in early childhood development, to maintain a ratio of one adult to every four children.

Ample time is provided for physical growth and developmental activities, but most of each center day is devoted to structured programs that speed and inspire educational, social and skills development. Statistics show a positive relationship between children who attend NCCC centers and their success in formal schooling.

Enrollment periods at NCCC coincide with local public school calendars. Summer programs are also available.

Industry Problems

With the growing demand for child-care centers, new centers have been opening at a rapid pace for several years. Unfortunately, some centers are not operated at the quality levels they should be. This has invited increased scrutiny by agencies in many states.

It is now much more difficult to get a license to operate a child-care facility. Inspections are much more frequent. Disciplinary actions against operators not in full compliance with state regulations have become much more common. In fact, most states show an increased inclination to close down centers that are repeat offenders.

The number of reported cases of sexual abuse or other forms of mistreatment of children is rising, some of which get broad news coverage. This has made parents much more careful about selecting a center for their children. And they are much more watchful than ever in the recent past.

NCCC generally is recognized as a model that others should copy. NCCC has never violated state regulations and has never had parents file a complaint about improper treatment of their children. But the poor image of the industry in general affects NCCC, which has redoubled its efforts to remain an industry leader.

Major Players at NCCC

The NCCC president is George P. Schuss. Schuss is a native Californian who came to NCCC two years ago. He holds degrees in operations management and law. In fact, his former law practice in Santa Barbara was noted for cases that involved children and social service agencies. Schuss is generally regarded as a leading authority on laws affecting daycare centers. He's also regarded as an efficient but people-sensitive manager.

Sully T. Trotter is vice president of marketing. "Sully" is short for Sullivan, a maternal family name. She has undergraduate and graduate degrees in advertising and marketing from the University of Illinois, Champaign. She joined the NCCC management team last year after spending the previous six years as director of market planning for Playschool, Inc., maker and distributor of a wide range of educational toys.

Shirley M. Kidd is vice president of program development. She has B.A., M.A. and Ph.D. degrees, all from the University of Kansas, in early childhood development, as well as an M.B.A. in management from Syracuse.

She's been with NCCC six years and is credited with innovative programs that have spurred NCCC's recent growth.

Terry Childers is vice president of communications. His B.A. in public relations and M.A. in advertising are from the University of Texas at Austin. Having served as an account supervisor for a major agency in New York City for four years, Terry returned to his native Dallas to join NCCC. He had also worked as an account representative in Dallas (two years) and Chicago (two years).

Major Players at BABY

BABY's corporate headquarters is Chicago, Ill. Its chief executive officer is Manford Z. Topper, who has been in this role since BABY was formed by its four principal investors 15 years ago. Topper had several successful years of brand management with Procter & Gamble, then moved to General Foods as vice president in charge of new product and market planning.

He is a lifelong friend and fraternity brother of Paul V. Betters. It was only natural that Betters and the other BABY principals would turn to Topper because of his stellar credentials. They sweetened the deal with Topper at the end of the first two years with 3 percent of BABY's stock. The rest of the stock was equally divided among the four principals until BABY went public three years ago. Topper and the other four still control 72 percent of BABY's stock.

BABY has four principals. Walter F. Armes is a physician from Corpus Christi, Tex., who made his fortune in real estate development. Paul V. Betters is a real estate developer in Chicago, Ill.

Harry U. Bottoms from Yonkers, N.Y., has principal holdings in two cruise lines, oil and gas exploration and distribution and food processing. He is also the principal stockholder in one of the nation's leading retail chains.

Juan Villareal Yema, an entrepreneur from Seattle, has large timber holdings and owns wood-processing plants in the Northwest. He is also a major stockholder in Sun Computers, a Silicon Valley company that wants to challenge IBM, Apple and Compaq in the office computers market.

Notes

Quick-Study

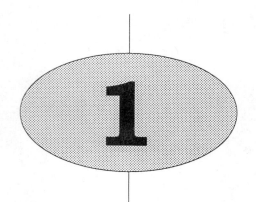

Extract, Chapter 1, "Public Relations and the Writer,"
Public Relations Writing: Form & Style 6e, Belmont, California: Wadsworth, 2001.

Y ou must first reconcile the two senses in which the term *public relations* is used. The *general sense* simply describes the art of getting along with people. The *professional sense* describes the art of *brokering goodwill* between an organization and its publics. Good writing usually plays a central role in the brokering process.

That is because good public relations writers play many roles. They must be able *to identify with priority or target publics*, adapt *appropriate writing styles*, write messages to *fit the format* of the media used to deliver them and shape their messages, without distortion, so that the messages are *acceptable* to target publics.

Be careful as a beginning writer to avoid the synonymous use of the terms *advertising*, *publicity* and *public relations*. They are not the same things, although the lines between them are blurred more than ever. The following points may help you sort out some main differences among these terms:

1. *Advertising is media time or space bought to carry and distribute the buyer's message.* In effect, buyers lease this time or space so that they can control what, when, how and how often messages go to target publics. It is communication in one direction.

2. *Publicity is information given without charge or payment to the media.* Its use, if any, is at the discretion of editors of the media, not yours. It is also one-way communication.

3. *Public relations communication is two-way communication* that may, and often does, use advertising and publicity, but public relations distinctly seeks the mutual benefits of interacting and exchanging information with mass and specialized media and publics. The media and public relations share a common goal: *to engage their*

respective publics in sustained relationships. Good writers are key players in these situations.

Publics are people tied together by common bonds. Understanding how and why these bonds are formed is a fundamental challenge to all writers. Research can uncover demographic and psychographic information that can help writers to understand attitudes, beliefs, values and behaviors. Without this understanding, they guess. They may guess wrong.

Good writers also know they must shape their messages one way for a particular public and in a different way for another public. Some publics are more important than others to their organizations. These are *priority* publics, and writers focus their messages on those groups. That process is called *targeting the message to the public.*

You must also tailor the message to the format of the medium used to deliver it to the target public. New media of importance are Web pages and CD-ROMs, and each can influence the way you construct messages, just as other media do. Of course, the medium not only must be able to carry the message but also must be one to which a public pays attention.

Good public relations writers also must intimately know the organizations they work for, the publics most important to their organizations and the channels of communication to which these publics pay the most attention. All of this is necessary to write effectively and efficiently in all appropriate media pertinent to publics. The first commandment of public relations writing is: *Know your public(s).*

A primary responsibility of the public relations writer is to broker good-will between an institution and its publics. This operates at two levels. The writer interprets *strategic decisions* that influence the face-to-face interaction of employees with customers or clients and the organization's participation in the affairs of the community. Good policies and good performance are worth little if people don't understand the policies and don't know about the performance. *Tactical success* remains at the heart of public relations practice, particularly writing.

All Scenarios 1 : 1

Review the scenario assigned to you or, if you are working independently, selected by you. Make a list of all the possible publics related to the scenario. Be as detailed as possible. Refer to Example 1:1 in *PRW6e* for help. Remember the rule from the Quick-Study: *Know your public(s)*. It is impossible to make the list too detailed. Then group the publics by type, such as government, which should be further divided into local, state and national. Having done that, now separate these publics into internal and external.

Independent 1 : 1

Do what's described above, but focus the list on the college you attend or attended. If you've been away from campus some time, select a profit or non-profit organization in your community and complete the exercise.

All Scenarios and Independent 1 : 2

Study your list from Assignment 1:1. Which of these publics is most important to the organization? Least important? The PVI information on page 12 in *PRW6e* will help you derive answers systematically. Rank-order the list so that the most important public is listed first, the second most important is listed second and so on. Write a brief but detailed report (three or four paragraphs) that explains why you listed these publics in that order.

All Scenarios and Independent 1 : 3

Refer to the public you listed as the most important in Assignment 1:2. Think about the people who make up that public. What holds them together as a group? What are they like as individuals? What do they do for a living? How do they spend their free time? What issues are important to them? Feel free to add your own questions. Write a summary memo of your conclusions about this public to Ms. Kari M. Backe, account services supervisor at ProCom. This is an important memo because the account team will review it later when the team prepares to write assignments for a client.

Notes

Quick-Study

Extract, Chapter 2, "Ethical and Legal Responsibilities of the PR Writer,"
Public Relations Writing: Form & Style 6e, Belmont, California: Wadsworth, 2001

Y ou must be sensitive to the feelings and needs of others, and treat them as you want to be treated by them. This sensitivity exerts its greatest influence in the way you and the organization for which you work perceive something as *right* or *wrong*. If these perceptions don't align generally with those of your relevant publics, *credibility* may be jeopardized. If you or your organization lose credibility, neither you nor your organization will be very successful.

The right or wrong of a situation may have little or nothing to do with facts or truth or what may be defined in laws, regulations or rules. That's because people's *perceptions are their realities*. Even if the *explicit messages* you write are factual and truthful, they may be contradicted by the *implicit messages* publics perceive in your organization's behavior.

Remember that how relevant publics perceive your organization is more likely to be based on the *consequences* of what your organization *does* than on what you *say* about it. If your organization operates outside the limits of your public's acceptable standards, what you say or do may make little difference to them. You have a special professional responsibility in such cases to reconcile these differences to the mutual benefit of your organization and its publics. That task often isn't easy.

Your personal and professional sense of ethical and socially responsible behavior plays a key role in how you perform as a writer. If you are in tune with the standards of your organization, the public relations industry and your public, you'll find your job easier. If you are out of step, your job will be more difficult.

Your real worth to your organization is knowing the limits of what its relevant publics view as acceptable behavior and staying well within them. You must make regular and sustained efforts to keep in touch with relevant publics. Only then can you expect to construct messages both valuable and acceptable to them.

You will work in a litigation-happy environment. You must protect yourself and your organization by bulletproofing your writing as much as possible. Legal actions can be brought at any time for any reason. So you may not always avoid them, but you can keep them from being successful. Pay particular attention to the laws of libel, slander, contracts, contempt, privacy and copyright. You should review the content of Examples 2.3 ("Red Flag Words") and 2.4 ("A Guide to Libel") in *PRW6e*. If you have doubts about how to say something or even if something should be said, consult an attorney who specializes in communication law.

Also keep up with rulings from the Postal Service, the Federal Trade Commission, the Securities and Exchange Commission or similar governmental bodies that deal with the industry of which your organization is a part.

One important point to remember about laws and regulations is that they are always in *flux*. What is legally and ethically permissible today may not be so tomorrow. Another is that laws are generally *negative*. They define what is not permissible, not what is permissible. Even if something is not prohibited by law, it still may be perceived as unethical. So being legal is not enough to sustain your success as a public relations writer. *You must be perceived as ethical and legal.*

Exercises Exercises **Exercises** Exercises

All Scenarios and Independent 2 : 1

The office of public information at State University yesterday, in response to persistent rumors during the last few days, confirmed that Melody S. Hanzout, daughter of U.S. Sen. Herchel H. Hanzout, has been awarded a full scholarship (tuition, fees, books, supplies, room and board) to finish her fifth year of study at the university. She has maintained a 3.6 grade point average (on a 4.0 scale) during her first four years of study.

The managing editor of the *Clarion* assigned a reporter to interview Ms. Hanzout because the Hanzout family is widely known around Serene.

Early in the interview Ms. Hanzout expressed some dismay at having gotten a scholarship, because she had never applied for one. This prompted the reporter to wonder why the scholarship had been awarded. Contacts were made with several people.

The president of the university, Dr. T.A. Lott, said that Ms. Hanzout was singled out as a deserving student, and the university simply wanted to acknowledge her scholarship. When asked if the scholarship award was made to win the favor of her father, a U.S. senator, Lott said, "Certainly not. We don't try to buy influence."

The director of student financial aid, Edgar M. Burns, said Ms. Hanzout deserved the scholarship not only for her scholarly record but also for her leadership as president last year of her sorority, Alpha Alpha Alpha. He pointed out she had also been active in a number of Greek activities throughout her tenure at the university.

When asked if it was common to award scholarships to students who had not applied, Burns said, "It has happened before, but not often. We try to make sure scholarship money goes to deserving applicants only." When asked who made the decision to award the scholarship, Burns said the decision was made "higher up" and the word came in a telephone conversation, but he couldn't remember from whom. Asked to name other students who had been given scholarships, he declined to say, indicating that privacy laws prevented such disclosures.

Several members of the scholarship application review committee denied any knowledge of the scholarship awarded to Ms. Hanzout. The chair, Professor Damon R. Philley, said she is appalled by the cavalier way the scholarship was awarded. She pledged that her committee would look into the matter immediately.

Sen. Hanzout was away from his Washington office on a fact-finding tour to the Middle East, but Hanzout's press aide, Montgomery (Monty) F. Peace, responded to phone questions from the *Clarion* reporter that Sen. Hanzout is proud of his daughter and her accomplishments and is especially pleased about her scholarship.

Sen. Hanzout was also reported to have said the university is a fine one and he's very glad his daughter is a student there. Peace also confirmed that Hanzout expects to be named chair of the U. S. Senate's education subcommittee next year. The current chairman has announced he will not seek office after his current term ends this year.

The story in yesterday's *Clarion* caused an uproar on campus. The chair of the university's faculty senate called an emergency meeting of the executive committee and at noon issued a strongly worded statement that condemned the university's action. The statement also carried a muted inference that Lott should resign from the presidency.

The executive committee of student government also met briefly and issued a similar statement. But the student government statement openly called for resignations from both Lott and Burns. Lott issued a prepared statement today at 1 P.M., the text of which reads:

> The scholarship awarded to Ms. Melody S. Hanzout was given in recognition of her outstanding scholastic record and her achievements as a leading citizen of the university community. It is the standing policy of the university to recognize students in many ways for their achievements. I am not sure personally who made the decision to award the scholarship, but it was a good decision. Because there seems to be some concern about it, my office today has launched an investigation into the process by which all scholarship decisions are made.

Lott today did not take or return phone calls from the media. Even when Burns took media calls, he responded to all questions with "No comment." Unconfirmed reports say several media representatives appear to be camped just outside the president's office.

Other than staff members, only two people, I.M. Professor and Ms. Kari M. Backe of ProCom, have been allowed into Lott's suite. Rumor has it that Lott called them in as consultants to assist him with the problem. A student protest march around the administration building at 4 P.M. today has been called by the student government president.

The phone rings at your desk at ProCom. It is Ms. Backe calling from Lott's office. She directs you to get together with the other writers at ProCom and research the situation at the university. "We're in Lott's office now. As you know, it has really hit the fan. We may be here well into the evening while we try to sort out strategic approaches to a solution to the problem. What Professor and I want you to do is to research the legal and ethical dimensions of the problem. Hit the law books and other sources and give us a summary of your findings. Your research may uncover other questions, but look at these for starters:

1. What legal requirements must be observed?

2. Is it better to try to cover up an unseemly situation than to face it squarely? What is the rationale for either decision?

3. What are the university's obligations to Ms. Hanzout and to its relevant publics, such as students, faculty and staff?

4. What ethical questions must be resolved?

5. Do ethical and legal issues conflict in this instance? If so, how can they be resolved?"

Then Backe directs you to write a two-page summary of relevant findings and have it ready for review at 7 A.M. tomorrow. "We'll finish the strategy discussion with Lott this afternoon or evening," she said, "but we won't implement anything until we've thoroughly studied your report. Your purpose is to keep us and Lott from making a serious mistake."

Notes

Quick-Study

Extract, Chapter 3, "Persuasion,"
Public Relations Writing: Form & Style 6e, Belmont, California: Wadsworth, 2001.

Persuading someone to adopt your point of view is difficult and complex. That's because behavior has rational and emotional dimensions. Being rational means people can think for themselves. Because of diversity in background and experience, other people's outlooks may differ from your own. That makes your job harder. Persuasion is your only recourse because you can't make audiences comply.

You must figure out how to persuade your publics that your way or view about an issue is sounder, clearer, more reasonable perhaps than another. That sounds simple, but it isn't. There are no surefire ways to persuade people, but a few guidelines may help.

Learn everything you can about human behavior. Remember, only a few basic persuasive strategies exist, although many variations of each one are possible. Choose the strategic approach best suited to your purpose. Always make this choice from the point of view of your public.

If your purpose is merely to gain simple awareness and association, a *stimulus-response* approach may work. If you're dealing with a sophisticated public likely to be skeptical of what you're saying, consider a *cognitive* strategy. If an appeal to a public's self-interest will meet your purpose, then a *motivational* approach may work, but only if you show your public a desirable reward.

If individuals in your target public identify strongly with group norms, a strategy based on *social* relationships may be best. A *personality* strategy may work if your target audience is made up of people who see themselves as real individualists. But this last strategy is hard to execute because it is difficult to make a message personal when it goes to millions. Consult Chapter 3 in *PRW6e* for detailed explanations of these strategies.

Even if you use the right strategy, you may fail if you don't pay attention to the steps in the persuasion process. If you skip a step, you're less effective. You must reach people at the *right time and place,* with the *right message* and in the *right form* if you expect publics to pay *attention.* They won't *understand* what you want them to know if you don't get their attention. And they may not *accept* what you say, even if they understand it completely. You also must *reinforce* their acceptance long enough for them to take the *action* you want.

How your organization presents an issue or program must match closely what you say about it. You lose *credibility* when actions and words don't coincide. You won't be believed. In fact, you may be mistrusted. Remember also that some media have more credibility than others.

Determine when and under what conditions you should give only your side of an issue. Other important decisions in the persuasion process include which side should be given first, whether the good or bad news should be shared first and whether an explicit conclusion is preferred over letting an audience draw its own.

Pay particular attention to how or even if you should appeal to your public's fears, especially in the context of social issues and political campaigns. And learn as much as you can about when it is best to use rational or emotional appeals or a combination of both.

The spoken word is generally more persuasive than the written word. But the written word seems to produce more understanding than the spoken. Opinion leaders are generally more media-dependent than most members of a public. Many persuasive efforts seen in the media are filtered through opinion leaders, so how the message influences the broader audience is often an indirect process. If you want to sensitize a public to an issue, you must get it on the public agenda through the media.

Time may be your best ally when your organization suffers a loss in public confidence. People tend to forget. This tendency also means that you must keep reminding people about your organization. If you do, it is easier to deal successfully with audiences when problems arise unexpectedly.

What you write begins with an implicit persuasive purpose. Disguising your intent may hamper the way you write and muddle your messages. What you gain in acceptance by disguising your purpose may be more than offset by losses in levels of attention and understanding.

All Scenarios and Independent 3 : 1

Review the situation described in Assignment 2:1. Dr. T.A. Lott, president of State University in Serene, had called in Professor and Backe from ProCom for advice on how to handle the problem of the scholarship awarded to Melody Hanzout.

Ms. Backe had asked you to provide a brief the next morning for her and the Professor to review before they gave the go-ahead to Lott on the strategy worked out the night before. Professor and Backe reviewed your brief and found nothing in it to suggest the chosen strategy would be a mistake. When Professor called Lott to give him the green light, President Lott became hostile. Some of his comments follow:

"You really expect me to say and do those things? Why, the students, faculty and alumni will crucify me and the university. I am the leader of this university. It has too many friends in positions of influence to allow harm to come to it. You people just don't know much about how the academic mind works."

"This is really just a tempest in a teapot. It will blow over soon. I should have followed my own judgment in the first place. I've turned the matter over to Mann (Y.S. Mann, director of information at the university) who knows how to do what I tell him."

"You can send me your invoice for the services you didn't render to me and I'll see about getting it paid—sometime." With that, President Lott hung up the phone. Professor leaned back and laughed loudly in disbelief.

Mann called a press conference at 11 A.M., at which time he issued a news release, quoted below.

Dr. T.A. Lott, president of State University, announced this morning that no consideration will be given to revoking the scholarship awarded to Melody S. Hanzout of Serene. The scholarship became the focus of protests yesterday by faculty and students when a *Clarion* reporter revealed Ms. Hanzout had not applied for a scholarship.

"This whole affair has been blown out of proportion by muckraking media and misguided people who really don't understand the nature of the university's scholarship program," Lott said.

President Lott has also called for a full investigation into the way applicants are evaluated and how scholarships are awarded.

"If mistakes in our scholarship program have been made, we must know about them so that we can correct them," he said.

"But under no circumstances will Melody's scholarship be rescinded," he continued, "because she's already suffered enough abuse at the hands of the media and insensitive supporters of the university."

A full investigation of the scholarship program will take two to three months to complete, said Y.S. Mann, director of information. "President Lott is eager to see the final report so that steps can be taken to prevent problems similar to this one," Mann said.

Mann then fielded questions from reporters for about five minutes. Some of his responses follow.

"No, Melody emphatically was not given the scholarship because of the potential influence her father can bring to bear on behalf of the university. That is patently absurd, and an insult to Sen. Hanzout and President Lott."

"Yes, Dr. Lott is very concerned about the whole affair and determined to resolve it quickly and equitably."

"No, Dr. Lott thinks it's funny that some people are calling for his scalp. And he certainly does not intend to give it to them willingly."

"Ms. Hanzout is an outstanding student whose record fully justifies the scholarship awarded to her. That she did not apply for it in no way means she does not deserve it. She represents the very kind of student the university seeks to recruit."

"Dr. Lott will make no further statements about this matter until the final report on the scholarship program evaluation is complete. Thank you for coming. If I can be of further help, call me."

Professor assigns you to review and analyze carefully the content of the university's news release and Mann's comments to reporters. "Even if ProCom is no longer related to this client," Professor explains, "you'll learn a lot about persuasion by looking at what is going on out there now. So write me a brief report (about two double-spaced pages) and have it on my desk tomorrow in time for our regular meeting." Professor goes on to suggest that, among others, the report should consider the following questions:

1. Which persuasive strategy(ies) is (are) most apparent in the news release and statements at the press conference? Explain why it (they) will or will not work.

2. Which step(s) in the persuasive process may be jeopardized most by the strategy(ies) used?

3. What other persuasive communication flaw(s) can you spot in the way Lott and Mann are handling this problem?

4. Is another strategic approach better? If so, which one, and why do you recommend it?

Notes

Quick-Study

Extract, Chapter 4, "Research for the Public Relations Writer,"
Public Relations Writing: Form & Style 6e, Belmont, California: Wadsworth, 2001.

Public relations writers depend on information generated from research. The less they know about something, the more they need research. The more they research something, the more likely they are to recognize what they don't know. Knowing what they don't know is the first step toward enlightenment. Filling those information gaps with credible data helps them avoid mistakes. You also must be aware that while computers made the search process easier they also made it a lot riskier. Be skeptical about what you choose to use.

Good writers know, at least instinctively, that they'll make more mistakes when they write about something that stretches the limits of their knowledge about a topic. Aside from topic-specific knowledge, the research most writers do focuses on six broad areas: policy, background material, public, message, media and program evaluation.

Research information is useless if it can't be retrieved quickly. That's why most writers form personal habits of routinely filing away information for later use. They also know where and how to get the needed information not already in their offices. They may spend a good bit of time in libraries poring over journals and reference books or gleaning information from flickering images on microfilm or microfiche readers. They also may dial electronic data bases and call up what they need. And the Internet has become a valuable source for a wide range of information, although its credibility is sometimes in doubt. Clearly, the source or form of the information is not as important as knowing where and how to get it.

The information needed in most public relations writing situations already exists. Searching existing information is called *secondary research*. It is secondary not because it is unimportant but because it was developed elsewhere for other purposes, and your potential use of it is secondary to its original intent.

Even when writers know that information is available, they sometimes don't recognize it when they see it. It is like wondering why utility hole covers in streets are round. Everyone who took geometry in high school knows why, but most people don't make the connection, at least immediately. A circular cover is the only shape that won't fall into the hole if it is dislodged by traffic. What's the point? Writers must be able to synthesize information. They must see relationships between seemingly unrelated concepts or data.

When information is not already available, you must do *primary research*. Its most common forms are interviews and surveys. However, you must still turn to secondary information to prepare carefully for the questions you do ask. Otherwise, your interview or survey won't elicit the information you need from your primary research. If you're not very familiar with the focus of a research question or you don't know much about a target public, do a focus group interview (FGI) before writing questions for an interview or survey. FGIs help you to learn the usual language a public uses. This helps you to sharpen questions in ways that are understood more clearly by a target public. Because the number of respondents in an FGI is very small—often about 10, you can't generalize from your findings. Even when you do several FGIs with a target public, the combined number is still small and is not statistically representative of the target public.

Secondary or primary data are often in statistical form, and much data have been developed from samples. If the sample was not randomly chosen and is not truly representative, then the data generated should not be generalized about your entire public.

Be skeptical if research protocols (noted in Example 4.4, *PRW6e*) are missing or are so vaguely worded you can't see exactly how the information was developed. It may be good information, but it also may be bad. Good writers cross-check information. Just because a source says something is true does not make it so. It is only when several sources generally say the same thing that you can be reasonably sure of the accuracy, meaning and reliability of the information.

One of the most common writing projects in PR is the *facts sheet*, a compendium of the findings from a range of continuing research efforts. Its value can be enormous if it is current, accurate and complete.

A special kind of research is what is known as a communication audit. This is a procedure intended to evaluate how information flows within an organization. It usually involves an analysis of secondary matter, such as letters, memos, brochures, etc. And it usually includes a broad-based survey of all employees, soliciting their reactions to the kinds of information they get from which sources and its utility. And in-depth personal interviews are common. These are usually done after secondary and primary information has been assembled. A well-executed audit yields a lot of information that is helpful to public relations writers but also to all levels of management who frequently initiate minor and major policy changes.

Exercises Exercises **Exercises** Exercises

GEI 4 : 1

Review scholarly and popular journals and newspapers for articles on molecular biology and DNA written in the last three years. Look especially for reports of new discoveries and new applications. Search for pieces that provide insights into such questions as:

1. Why did it take so long for scientists to map the first genome?
2. Is it likely that humans can be cloned like sheep? Identify the pro and con arguments.
3. What do scientists speculate are the causes of mutations?
4. What are some of the legal, ethical, philosophical and religious problems that must be resolved when considering the cloning of humans?
5. Which of the problems mentioned in four above is most likely to directly affect the work at GEI? Why do you believe this?

Write a report of no more than four pages, typed or word-processed and double-spaced, summarizing your findings.

NATS 4 : 1

Review scholarly and trade journals, as well as popular journals, of the last three years that deal with the medical profession in general and emergency medicine specifically. Search for articles and reports that describe the kinds of problems faced by institutions and people specializing in giving emergency care. Look for information that gives insights into issues such as:

1. Reasons why emergency care costs are skyrocketing.

2. Patterns of behavior of emergency medicine caregivers.

3. Effects of malpractice suits, not just on costs but also on policies, on institutions and on the related behavior of emergency medicine caregivers.

4. Problems related to getting more physicians to specialize in emergency medicine.

Write a report of no more than four pages, typed or word-processed and double-spaced, summarizing your findings.

NCCC 4 : 1

Research the scholarly and trade literature of the last three years that deals with day-care trends and developments. Look especially for information that gives insights into such issues as:

1. The growing need for day-care programs and facilities.

2. Which factors are most important in predicting trends in the day-care industry.

3. Why entrepreneurs have entered the day-care business.

4. How child development programs can be integrated into day-care services.

5. What kinds of staff credentials must be sought if developmental programs are part of day-care operations.

Write a report of no more than four pages, typed or word-processed and double-spaced, summarizing your findings.

Independent 4 : 1

Read scholarly and trade journals of the last three years that deal with scholarship and financial aids programs in higher education. Also get as much information as you can from the scholarship and financial aids office at your own university. Treat this information as if it is from the scholarships and financial aids office at Serene's State University. Also review the scholarship situation at State University as described in Assignments 2:1 and 3:1. Write a report on the status of the scholarship and financial aids programs at State University, paying special attention to such issues as:

1. University-wide scholarship policies.

2. Criteria for certain scholarships imposed by donors.

3. How and to what extent equity is maintained throughout the scholarship program.

4. Whether the scholarship and financial aids program at State University is adequate to support students who must have help to get through their degree programs.

5. The level of confidence faculty, staff, students and donors have in the way the scholarship and financial program is administered.

Write a report of no more than four pages, typed or word-processed and double-spaced, summarizing your findings.

All Scenarios and Independent 4 : 2

Consider the research report prepared in Assignment 4:1. Write a two-page, typed or word-processed, double-spaced report that describes what you believe may be important information that you could not find. Suggest where this information might be found and how you propose to get it.

All Scenarios and Independent 4 : 2 (Alternate)

Communication audits are done every two or three years by organizations interested in knowing how to improve the flow of information between management and employees. These audits represent an extensive, intensive self-analysis that may uncover troublesome bottlenecks that impede flow, identify good and bad practices, show what sources employees rely on most and which sources have the greatest credibility. Management can use this information to modify procedures or create new policies that improve communication within an organization. Consider the scenario you are working on. Write a two-page, typewritten or word-processed, double-spaced report in which you identify the major components of a communication audit, such as personal interviews, surveys, etc. Under each component, justify why that component should be in the audit. Describe also what kind of information you expect the audit to reveal and how that information may be useful.

Notes

Quick-Study

5

Extract, Chapter 5, "Writing to Clarify and Simplify the Complex: Style and Content," *Public Relations Writing: Form & Style* 6e, Belmont, California: Wadsworth, 2001.

A public relations writer rarely writes messages that are required reading, viewing or listening by target publics. The importance of that point is that target publics are made up mostly of people who are volunteer readers, viewers or listeners. Volunteers don't want to struggle to figure out what you want them to know. You must clarify and simplify. The art of clarifying and simplifying begins with three simple rules:

1. Know your message.
2. Know your public(s).
3. Know which medium your public is most likely to pay attention to.

If you can't write a simple, declarative sentence that explains the crux of your message, stop and think about it some more. When you know exactly what is the message, then write it from the public's point of view. In effect, you must figure out how to let the public have your way about something. Shape the message to conform to your public's expectations and needs. Craft it to fit the medium used to deliver it.

These rules suggest how to think about writing, not how to write. Other rules apply to the art of writing. For example, write about two or three grade levels below the average of your public's reading level. Remember that they are volunteers. They don't want to stand on their intellectual tiptoes to figure out what you are trying to say. This is not a suggestion that you write down to your target public, but merely that you write your message so it is more likely to be read, seen or listened to. Make it a practice to do a readability analysis of what you write. An analysis of this abstract showed an average sentence length of 13 words. The reading-ease score means that about 60.9 percent of all adults can read the abstract without difficulty. Readability is at the 8.9 grade reading level.

Writing that impresses people is writing they can understand with relative ease. Remember that usually you can't command a target public to read, view or listen. Your only choice is to write so people will volunteer their attention and time. Some software programs can do a readability analysis for you. It is easy. It is a good idea to look carefully at the readability formulas in Appendix A, PRW6e. Each focuses on average sentence and word lengths. Your appreciation of what the computer can do for you will be helped if you do at least one readability analysis by hand. People generally read more if you write with sentences that average about 14 to 17 words. Short, familiar words also get more attention and understanding.

Clarity is requisite, but good *style* is important also. Even if you write clearly, a dull style can put people to sleep, and your message may be lost. If motivation is very high, some people will wade through the worst of writing for bits of information they want. But most volunteers aren't driven to that level of effort. Besides short sentence and word lengths, you must try for *naturalness*. This is writing style that is conversational in tone. It exudes a feeling that you may get when talking to a good friend. *Variety* also helps. Vary grammatical structures, word choices and sentence lengths. A monotonous style can make clear writing so boring that people tune out. *Euphony* is another important influence. Writing that is rhythmic and makes good use of figures of speech is more enjoyable to read than stilted prose. The best way to develop a good sense of euphony is to read and study good writers. *Human interest* also helps make writing more inviting. Messages about people have explicit human interest. But writing about something mechanical, impersonal or abstract can be a challenge to build in human interest. Avoid *trite expressions* that make your writing sound old. Also remember that careless word choices can be unintentionally disparaging to groups of people—very old and very young, ethnic minorities and women. Adopt a *gender-neutral* style, and write with sensitivity to the feelings of people of all types.

One of the great challenges in public relations writing today is to write simply about complex topics. The rapid growth of scientific and technology-based information makes your job more difficult every day, but don't despair because you can simplify the complex by following a few simple rules.

Knowing your subject is foremost. That means you'll have to do some research—a lot, sometimes—on the topic because your target public can't understand the message if you don't. *Jargon words* are often part of complex topics. These must be understood clearly or you'll make some serious mistakes that may mislead your target public. That can be fatal. You must remember always to *use plain English* because that's what most people understand. That's what they expect and yearn for when they're reading outside of their field. Using plain English also means that you avoid *doublespeak*. Doublespeak generally intends to impress, not to communicate. *Euphemisms* are favorite devices in doublespeak. This tactic substitutes a "pleasant" word or phrase for a more resolute one. For example, "She passed away" rather than "She died." Listen to politicians for lessons on how to use euphemisms. That can teach you a lot about what not to do as a writer.

Use simple rather than *fancy words*. Fancy words often inflate you writing and sometimes obscure its meaning. *Gobbledygook* is a linguistic legacy of bureaucracy. It is bureaucratese written large and often. It favors phrases like "parameters to work within" when "specific limits" is plainer, simpler and easier to understand. It is also important to *describe, don't define*. Using technically correct definitions may show that you know your topic, but your mission is to communicate. You can do that best by describing concepts in terms people understand. Develop your descriptive powers to a high order. You should also take *one step at a time*. Build your message around small bits of information that flow logically and easily. Telling people too much too quickly can result in information overload. They may not be able to identify the main point of the message. That brings up another point: *make the central point clear*. Tell people at the beginning what is your point. This gives them a context in which to evaluate what you say later. It also imparts a sense of anticipation about what follows. Finally, remember to *explain the unfamiliar with the familiar*. Study Example 5.5 in *PRW6e*. It shows how analogy can reduce a complex idea to a level that most people can understand.

Study the message about writing by Martin Wank in Example 5.1, beginning on the next page. If you do the assignments in this chapter as well as they should be done, you will have learned more about clarifying and simplifying the complex than anything else you can do that requires the same amount of time.

Example 5:1

Martin Wank is president of Wank Associates in Greenvale, New York. His comments reflect a plea expressed more and more often. Take with utter seriousness the necessity of learning to write well.

Source: *Advertising Age*, February 18, 1991, p. 25. Used with permission of Martin Wank.

Wanted: Writers Who Can Write

By Martin Wank

Writing is a big part of the public relations profession. But agencies and companies seeking writers face an almost insurmountable challenge these days. What goes by the name of writer is usually a dreaming wanderer lost in a maze of meaningless words. There are many aspirants but few accomplished candidates.

One job candidate told me that the baby-boom generation, of which she was a part, never learned anything about writing in college. When I countered that my agency's work required thinking even more than writing, she laughed and said her generation knew less about thinking than about writing (herself excepted).

Two employees we hired and fired last year were graduates of the master's degree program in technology writing given by a well-known technical university in New York City. One had an undergraduate degree in mathematics. These candidates are just for us, I had thought, since we specialize in high technology, so we hired them. But we found that they could not write anything beyond a form of vernacular that imitated speech among their peers. Loose phrases used in everyday life appeared routinely in their copy—but it was not copy; that word should be reserved

> " . . . They believe that they are hired to write what they like, which should be sufficient to fill the bill. Only they don't know what the 'bill' is . . . "

for professional writing. In addition, they knew absolutely nothing about the business world and could not seem to get straight what factories do within their walls. They knew that products were manufactured there; how was a mystery, even though that knowledge was essential to our work.

One of the employees, a man about 30 years old, was on the way to becoming a carbon copy of Melville's "Bartleby the Scrivener" when he was fired. He took pleasure in hanging around the office, but did not work beyond constantly perusing papers. (He often wrote the redundant formulation: "perusing through . . . ") When I told him the jig was up, he said nothing. When I stood up to usher him out, he remained seated. When I opened the door as an invitation to leave, he remained as he was.

Example 5:1, continued —

Later, I interviewed a writing teacher from the undergraduate faculty of the same university. I told him about these two past employees and let them off easy by saying that they had studied on the graduate level. Not much difference, the teacher said. The undergraduates are terrible writers and are no better when they leave than when they arrive. He was not surprised that a master's degree in writing from his institution did not improve their skills.

What ails the supposed writers in our business, or those who are trying to get into our business? They know nothing about the structure of a piece of writing and have no idea that a piece of writing contains a structure. (Some of them have been taught a bit about forms—the interview, the inverted pyramid—but nothing about internal structure.)

They believe that writing is simply a progression from whatever beginning they choose to whenever they run out of gas. Running out of gas constitutes the end of the piece. After 10 years of searching, I have seen virtually no one who deigns to pen a conclusion—what one job candidate brightly termed "a kicker."

They do not know that a piece of writing has to have a forceful point, however much the force may be hidden from view. They resist absolutely writing what is needed; they believe that they are hired to write what they like, which should be sufficient to fill the bill. Only they do not know what the " bill" is; that is, the purpose of the piece they are trying to write—even though you will tell them over and over and prepare them and instruct them in every conceivable way, showing them countless examples of what is expected.

> "They know nothing about the structure of a piece of writing and have no idea that a piece of writing has a structure."

When you instruct them, I have found, they mentally look out the window. Their minds are turned off. They are at the beach if it is summer, skiing if it is winter. They are also mildly amused at the entire instruction process, as though they were observers, not participants.

There has been a flurry of books about failing education systems in the U.S., and American's weakened economic position in the world, and how these two are related. Believe it. If what I have seen in trying to recruit writers (for what is after all a small public relations agency) reflects what is happening out there, we are just at the beginning of the bad news. Somebody up there does not want to tell us the whole truth all at once.

Exercises Exercises **Exercises** Exercises

All Scenarios and Independent 5 : 1

Improving your descriptive powers is essential if you want to become a good writer. Being able to describe something clearly and effectively depends on being a keen observer. Think of the times you've laughed or cried, felt relieved or apprehensive, excited or depressed. What happened to cause those feelings? Can you describe them to others so that they become "real"? Good writers can. To stretch your descriptive powers, write a paragraph of no more than 50 words for each of the ideas or concepts below. Your purpose is to make readers feel, taste, smell or see what you describe.

1. The touch of a just-bathed human body.
2. The scent of a rosebud (any color) in the early morning.
3. The taste of double chocolate mocha (or your favorite flavor) ice cream.
4. The smell of a new car's interior.

GEI 5 : 2

On the facing page is a brief description of the basic ideas surrounding the work of biological scientists. It is written at about the 16th grade level. A college senior should read and understand it with little effort. Study the underlined jargon words and concepts. Go to the library or search the Internet to see what you can find out about them. When you feel you understand them, rewrite the description as a one-page, typed or word-processed, double-spaced report about the work of biologists. Your report will be duplicated and distributed Wednesday to an 11th grade life sciences class at Serene High School. Remember your audience, and write to its level. Thus, lower the reading skill level to that of a ninth grade student. Write it right and simply. Consult Appendix A in *PRW6e* to learn how to do a readability analysis of your writing. You'll probably use the Flesch or Gunning Method. Identify the method used, and show your calculations on the back of your report.

Biologists, like other scientists, observe phenomena and make statements about them. If what they observe seems to exist in reality, they use one of two methods to establish order in what they observe. The <u>order-analytical</u> method tries to compare <u>structures</u> or <u>organisms</u> with each other and with <u>fossil remains</u> so that similarities and differences can be noted. The <u>cause-effect</u> method relies on experiments to show connections that may help establish scientific order.

The oldest method is the order-analytical method and is fundamental to <u>taxonomy</u>, <u>comparative physiology</u> and <u>biochemistry</u>. But the experimental method has been used most in the 20th century. It attempts to verify by experiments what has been <u>hypothesized</u> about a phenomenon.

Scientists don't agree as to which method is the most powerful or useful. Some argue that the cause-effect method is the only one that can lead to new <u>biological laws</u>. Adherents to the order-analytical method say that method is just as valid because it can lead to the development of a new <u>taxonomic system</u>, which can suggest the existence of evolution.

There are two broad schools of philosophy in biology. The <u>mechanism</u> perspective is that all life processes are physical and chemical. If mechanists can't express and explain behavior in physical and chemical terms, this failure is not seen as a weakness of the perspective but rather as a commentary on current scientific ignorance which they expect to correct with new information. On the other hand, <u>vitalism</u> holds that life has some characteristics that are unique to itself and that are not present in any <u>inorganic system</u>.

NATS 5 : 2

Ms. Louise Cooper teaches health education to seniors at Serene High School. She's assembling information for her course from many sources, including information about emergency medicine and cardiopulmonary resuscitation (CPR). Because NATS is headquartered in Serene, she has asked you to write a one-page, typed or word-processed, double-spaced summary she can duplicate and give to her students. A quick search in the files turns up the following copy. You check it and find it is written at about the 17th grade level, so you know it must be rewritten completely for her use. Because it will be given to high school seniors, you decide to rewrite it at the 10th grade level. Consult Appendix A in *PRW6e* for ways to do readability analyses of your writing. You'll probably use the Gunning or Flesch Method. Show the method used and your calculations on the back of your report.

<u>Emergency medicine</u> continues to grow. But it did not become a <u>board-certified speciality</u> until 1979. Emergency medicine seeks to prevent and treat <u>trauma</u> of all types. About 80 million people were treated in 1999 for trauma in the <u>emergency rooms</u> of about 5,400 hospitals in the United States. This treatment used the services of about 15,000 <u>emergency medicine physicians</u>; 300,000 <u>emergency medicine technicians</u>; 30,000

intermediate emergency medical technicians; 40,000 paramedics; 80,000 emergency room nurses; and about 90 hospital-based helicopter transport systems.

An important treatment procedure used with many trauma patients is cardiopulmonary resuscitation (CPR). This treatment evolved when artificial ventilation was combined with the older technique of chest compression, sometimes called closed chest cardiac massage. Medical researchers don't agree on what makes CPR a viable emergency treatment in some situations. But they continue to search for more effective methods, such as changing the relationship of ventilations to compressions or adding intermittent abdominal counterpulsations, but improvements have yet to change the basic CPR guidelines in use since the 1960s.

CPR is a temporary measure used until external cardiac defibrillation can be given. The quicker defibrillation is provided, the more successful the result. Automatic defibrillators are becoming common. Now there are portable units the size of a hardback book and so easy to operate that anyone can use them. Forecasters say these units may become as common as fire extinguishers in public gathering places. Most commerical airlines now have defibrillators on their planes.

NCCC 5 : 2

Ms. Backe finishes going through the morning's mail and asks you to come to her office as soon as possible. You save and close the word-processing file you're working on and enter her office. She hands you a letter from Sully Trotter, for whom you've been working on a brochure. Attached to the letter is a second sheet of information.

"I want you to handle Sully's request, and I'll need it before you leave work today," Backe says. You read the letter and the information attached. Trotter's letter is complimentary of the overall concept of the brochure and design and most of its copy. But Sully points out that the clients and potential clients of NCCC services represent a broad range of educational levels. At least one parent in most client households has a college degree. Many others have some college. A few have only high school diplomas. The average number of years of school is 13 for the least-educated spouse in client and potential-client households.

The letter says that NCCC believes strongly in the need for pre-enrollment evaluations of preschool children. NCCC also believes it is important that all parents of clients and potential clients understand completely what is involved in these evaluations. Sully notes that the copy section below is written at about the 17th grade level. "Although some of our clients can easily understand it, most can't," she says. "Please rewrite this section at about the 11th grade level. Surely, you have a writer at ProCom who can clean up this educationese."

As you prepare to rewrite this material, look hard at the underlined jargon words. Make sure you understand them fully before you start writing. Your rewrite must fit the space provided in the brochure's design. Plan on 225 to 250 words. Consult Appendix A in *PRW6e* for ways to test the level of your writing. When you finish, write on the back of your copy the name of the method used to check readability, and show your calculations.

Most preschool children conceive of themselves and others in simple <u>evaluative</u>, <u>concrete</u> terms. They construct their realities in rigid "good" and "bad" zones. They react to the <u>interpersonal behavior</u> of others and events <u>egocentrically</u> as they <u>internalize</u> how these behaviors and events may affect them. Because their <u>life experiences</u> are limited and they of-ten can't <u>articulate</u> their thoughts well, preschoolers are somewhat trapped in the present and must treat each situation as an isolated incident in which the actions and beliefs of others are unpredictable.

They perceive of <u>covert variables</u>, such as <u>emotion</u> or <u>motive</u>, as <u>rudimentary</u>, <u>global</u> and <u>rigid</u>. Their evalu-ations of others are greatly <u>biased</u> by immediate and observed events and behaviors, and they find it diffi-cult to relate one <u>conceptual dimension</u> to another. This makes it difficult for them to deal simulta-neously with <u>multiple cues</u> or to <u>integrate sequential</u> or <u>inconsistent </u>information. Preschool children also may confuse the <u>temporal</u> and <u>sequential</u> dimensions of events, and they often mix wishful thinking with facts. They are inclined to dwell on events that em-phasize pleasures and sorrows, rather than on a broader range of emotions.

A primary technique of evaluating preschool children is to observe them while they engage in play. Special attention is given to the <u>characteristics of play</u>, such as its <u>initiation</u>, <u>energy expended</u>, <u>manipulative actions</u>, <u>tempo</u>, <u>body movements</u>, <u>tone</u>, <u>integration</u>, <u>creativity</u> and how children <u>relate</u> to other people

during play. Evaluators look for <u>behavioral evidence</u>
regarding <u>persistence</u>, <u>orderliness</u>, <u>ingenuity</u>, <u>competi-</u>
<u>tiveness</u>, <u>closure</u> and <u>intensity of play</u>.

NCCC believes preschool assessments are necessary to
its success at grouping children according to <u>levels</u>
<u>of development</u>.

Independent 5 : 2

Select one of the three readability exercises in this unit for GEI, NATS or NCCC, and do the assignment as if you are handling that account.

Notes

Quick-Study

6

Extract, Chapter 6, "Grammar, Spelling and Punctuation,"
Public Relations Writing: Form & Style 6e, Belmont, California: Wadsworth, 2001.

Some people believe you "should write like you talk." There's some merit in this belief because good writing sounds conversational. But this view is used sometimes as an excuse for breaking every known rule of good grammar. It may be true that rules are substitutes for thought, but there lies the great strength of rules. People will understand more quickly if you write by the rules. If you don't, most people may not stop to think about your meaning. They'll just direct their attention elsewhere.

You learned as a child that sentences are formed by arranging subjects, verbs and objects in that general order. And you also learned that some punctuation marks serve as the traffic lights of grammar. You may get maimed or killed if you run a red light in your car. The meaning of what you write may suffer similar semantic harm if you violate grammar's common rules. It also is foolhardy to mix chemicals indiscriminately because they may blow you to smithereens. If you carelessly mix words and phrases, your writing may explode in your face. Good writers work hard to produce explosions of understanding, not misunderstanding.

Some writers fall into a trap if they try too hard to economize with words. Although tight writing is expected in public relations, it can lead to *ambiguity*. What you write may be ambiguous if you leave out "that" or use "which" instead of "that." This is especially true if you favor "which" clauses. Ambiguity also creeps in when subjects and verbs don't agree, when you don't know whether something is singular or plural. Although "data" is the plural of "datum," current usage accepts "data" as plural or singular. Such plurals as "media" for "medium" are standard usage, but "medias" and "mediums" are not. Therefore, the word *media* requires a plural verb; the word *medium*, a singular. Commas that set off phrases also can cause confusion. "Terry Blasi, and other students, are going to class at 11 A.M." Just delete the set-off phrase and write "Terry Blasi is going to class at 11 A.M."

One *myth of grammar* is that the word *none* is less than one, so it must be singular. Dictionaries generally say *none* is plural. And that's the way most people use it when they talk. Look hard at the rules for the use of "I" and "me." One rule says that you shouldn't split infinitives, and that's generally a good idea. But you may cause some confusion if you follow it blindly. Let the situation be your guide. Usually, you should avoid ending sentences with prepositions, but, like the rule on split infinitives, this is an influence from Latin purists who have handed it down over the centuries. If a sentence sounds better with a preposition at the end, write it that way.

Always keep a good grammar or language usage manual handy. But remember that such books are nothing more than collections of conventional practices. They can't answer every question. At best they may suggest only guidelines. And when you're writing messages for distribution through the mass media, you must conform to the style manuals those media use, despite what *your* manual says. Remember also that active voice is preferred, although passive may be better in some situations. Let circumstances dictate which one.

Spelling errors can quickly kill the effectiveness of otherwise good writing. Poor spelling casts doubt on your ideas. There is no dishonor in being a poor speller. Dishonor comes only from not recognizing the problem and doing something about it. Consult an authoritative dictionary often. If you're writing on a word processor equipped with a spell-check program, use it. And be sensitive to word choices. The wrong word spelled correctly is still the wrong word. If your word processor has a grammar-check program, use it too, but don't expect much help from it if you are already a fairly skillful writer.

You must also be sensitive to the use of global English. All English is not the same. Nor is spelling, punctuation and, in some instances, grammar. Should you use British- or American-English? They can be quite different. Use what is accepted and familiar to your public, not necessarily to you. Many words in British-English use an "s" instead of a "z." And there are other differences. For example, British-English uses single quotes instead of double, and periods, commas and other marks appear outside of quotations. Many words common in American-English are not the same in British-English. For example, an elevator is a "lift." The word processing program on your computer probably can be set to default to either American- or British-English.

Example 6 : 1

Why We Write It the Way We Do

Revamping The Post's stylebook sets off another war of the words.

by Thomas W. Lippman

Is *sitcom* a word? How about *fax*? *Rif*? Should *The Washington Post* use *gays* for *homosexuals*? What is the possessive of *boss*? What kinds of practitioners should be accorded the title *Dr.*? Are adherents of Islam to be called *Moslems* or *Muslims*? Should we print home addresses of victims and suspects in crime stories? Is *first lady* capitalized? Is the patch of greenery opposite the White House called *Lafayette Park* or *Lafayette Square*?

If you have quick and easy answers to these questions, perhaps you should have been the one to undertake the exhausting and sometimes divisive task we have just completed in The Washington Post newsroom: compilation of a new stylebook.

Every major newspaper has a stylebook. It sets out the newspaper's rules and preferences on usage, grammar, spelling, punctuation and abbreviation, but it is also a policy document, a document that specifies how the newspaper is going to communicate with its public on sensitive matters of taste, race, sexual preference, privacy, politics and religion.

Some words are labels. Some words convey approval or disapproval when, in fact, the newspaper does not wish to convey either. *Ultra-orthodox, radical, pro-life, reform, Indian, girl*—these are words we may hear every day without

taking offense, but they and hundreds of other words must be used cautiously in a newspaper read by people who have strong views about matters political, religious, racial and sexual—as well as grammatical.

At *The Washington Post* we know people care deeply about the words we use because our files are thick with letters—hurt letters, angry letters, funny letters, sarcastic letters—about every verbal topic from the punctuation of compound modifiers to the identification of juveniles in crime stories. "Dear Mr. Bradley," a pained reader wrote to Emeritus Editor Benjamin C. Bradlee, "I do not mean this letter to sound petty, because all writers make mistakes in grammar and syntax from time to time. Writers for *The Post*, however, are making a LOT of mistakes." His complaint? A columnist had observed that one course of action was "more preferable" to another.

A reader in Bethesda, Md., has besieged *Post* executives for years with complaints about our use of the apostrophe alone to form the possessive of words ending in "s" (*boss'*) rather than (*boss's*). Lawyers for large corporations are constantly reminding us that their trade names are protected by copyright and should not be used as generic terms. Optometrists and clinical psy-

Example 6 : 1, continued —

chologists hate it when we call someone with an MD degree "Dr." but deny the title to them. "A medical doctor neither has nor deserves a monopoly on the title 'Doctor' and the public should not be led to believe otherwise," we were told by Don H. Vater, "chairperson" of the D.C. Board of Optometry.

Islamic scholars beg to inform us that the name of the prophet should be spelled *Muhammad*. The National Sheriffs' Association says prison guards shouldn't be called *guards*, they are *corrections officers*. We have heard from a retired ordnance officer who argued at great length that we should use the spelling *fuze*, not *fuse*, and from an amateur astronomer who says the adjective from Venus is *Venerean*, not *Venusian*. A disabled lawyer called us "reactionary and obtuse" because we said someone was *confined to a wheelchair*. A man from Waldorf, Md., says we should use the term *birth mother* instead of *natural mother* in stories about adoption.

Nor are the arguments only between the news staff and our readers. Within this newsroom, the stylebook project touched off strenuous disagreements, mostly between purists and pragmatists on such subjects as the use of accent marks. (The purists insist on using accent marks and diacritical marks such as the tilde and the cedilla—"They're part of the spelling." The pragmatists say we should forget them because we don't know what they mean and, besides, it's too difficult to typeset them on deadline.) Some of our writers and editors seem to have developed bizarre

fetishes about the double "p" in *kidnapped* or the use of *author* as a verb or the correct sequence of tenses. We still have absolutists who insist that *none* always takes a singular verb and that an infinitive must never be split. They learned it a certain way in fifth grade, by George, so that's the way it has to be.

We don't have time to have these arguments on deadline. *The Washington Post* contains about 150,000 words on an average weekday, more than a 250-page book, and most of those words are written, edited and printed in about 12 hours. Do we call a Catholic priest *father*? Do we capitalize *cabinet*? Do we abbreviate *association*? Does a headline have to have a verb? There isn't time for long discussion. The stylebook is supposed to settle it. The purpose of a stylebook is to supplement the dictionary and ensure that our presentation is consistent and clear as well as accurate and tasteful.

At a newspaper, the word *style* has two meanings: the rules of punctuation, grammar, capitalization and usage that we apply to our written output, and the overall tone or approach. Obviously no single tone or style of writing is appropriate for every article in a publication that reports about every subject, cosmic or trivial, tragic or humorous. Our writing style will change with the material.

But our technical style should not. We are a medium of mass communication. The need to communicate clearly and quickly with a vast and diverse audience imposes its own restriction. We have little room for Joycean experi-

Example 6 : 1, continued —

mentation or 800-word, punctuation-free Faulknerian paragraphs. We strive for consistency of presentation not because we adhere pedantically to inflexible rules, but because we want to enlighten our readers without confusing them or diverting their attention from the material at hand. In addition, we recognize that the newspaper is read every day by people who expect us to uphold a high standard of English usage. Consistency of style is part of the high quality they have a right to demand.

Our current stylebook is more than 10 years old. It has been clear for some time that we needed a new one. Much has changed in the English language and in the Washington area since the mid-1970s, and in any case our copy editors found the stylebook's format, arranged by topic rather than alphabetically, hard to use. When I inherited the project a year ago from a senior editor who had retired, I greatly underestimated the difficulty of compiling a book that everyone would accept. The editors of the various sections of this paper exercise considerable autonomy, and I knew that if the stylebook laid down "rules" that editors found unworkable, they would ignore them.

For the sake of simplicity and consistency, I adopted the principle that we would deviate from the dictionary in spelling and capitalization only when there was some compelling reason to do so. But that raised new questions. The dictionary we use, *Webster's New World*, disclaims any judgmental role and thus tolerates spelling and usage that we find unacceptable.

"It is not the business of a dictionary either to give direction or to uphold pure standards" but to record the way people use the language, proclaims the preface to the third edition, published last year. That explains why linguistic atrocities such as *straightjacket* and *imposter* are "in the dictionary." But we don't want them in the newspaper. To resolve this difficulty, I adopted a rule developed by the Associated Press for its stylebook. Where more than one spelling is given, we will use the first or the one for which a full definition is given. That gives us *doughnut*, not *donut*, although the latter is "in the dictionary."

If only every decision had been so easy. It took several days and many exchanges of memos to agree on which reference work would be our primary source for place names. (We chose the *National Geographic Atlas of the World*.) Editors in the Food section lobbied for an exception from our overall style on weights and measures to accommodate their style on recipes. In the end, the most difficult decision turned out to be the one on using the title *Dr.*

The Washington Post calls most individuals by their names only: *John Smith* on first reference, *Smith* on subsequent references. *Mary Brown* on first reference, *Brown* thereafter. But the names of some people—members of the armed forces, holders of elected office, members of the clergy, professors—are preceded by the abbreviation of their title or an honorific: *Adm. John Smith, Sen. Mary Brown, the Rev. James White* and so

Example 6 : 1, continued —

on. Doctors are in this group. But who is a doctor?

Other titles are easy. The Navy tells us who is an admiral. A university tells us who is a professor. But who would tell us who gets the title *Dr.*?

The old stylebook said, "Use the title *Dr.* for practitioners of the healing arts (including chiropractors and osteopaths) but not for holders of PhDs or honorary degrees." Not much help there. Does that include veterinarians? Podiatrists? Pharmacists? And what about clinical psychologists, who treat patients but often hold PhD degrees?

In the vigorous debate over this, traditionalists argued that when people think of a doctor, they think of someone who holds an MD degree. But dentists and osteopaths are doctors, too. And what about those research scientists who are on the cutting edge of progress in fighting illnesses such as AIDS and cancer? Many of them have PhDs, but they certainly are "practitioners of the healing arts" and their colleagues call them *Dr.*

In the end, we adopted a radical solution that will give equal treatment to everyone who wants to be known as doctor: We decided to abolish the title. We will identify practitioners by their role, not their title: *John Smith, a cardiologist; Mary Brown, a biochemist; William Jones, a podiatrist.* You, the readers, can decide which of these practitioners you want to call *Dr.* We will not make that decision for you. We will use the word *doctor* as the generic term for an MD, but we will not use the title.

The answers we gave for the other linguistic questions asked above will become clear as we implement the new stylebook this spring. I have no doubt that some readers will disagree with whatever we decide, but they should be assured in advance that these decisions weren't made lightly. I don't expect the flow of letters to decrease, but it's likely that we'll start hearing from different people.

Source: *The Washington Post* (National Weekly Edition), March 27-April 2, 1989, p. 25. Copyright 1989, *The Washington Post.* Reprinted with permission.

Exercises Exercises **Exercises** Exercises

All Scenarios 6 : 1

ProCom has a style manual for its publications and promotional pieces. But when ProCom produces materials for a client, it uses the client's style. When it takes on a new client, ProCom's standard practice is to review the new client's style manual. If the client does not have one, ProCom studies the client's needs and recommends a particular style. Once the client agrees, ProCom employees faithfully follow that style. The problem confronting you now is that the client to which you are assigned—GEI, NCCC or NATS—does not have a style manual. Your assignment is to develop one for that client.

This assignment requires you to consider a wide range of style issues. Most client style manuals are built on the Associated Press style manual, especially for clients that produce lots of materials for distribution to the mass media. Often an organization will have three style manuals. One is an internal organizational style manual that details precisely how people will be addressed in letters, memos and the like. Another is a manual used to produce consistency in company newsletters, employee magazines and the like. Yet another is the style used when producing news releases and other materials to be distributed to the mass media. Here are some suggestions to help you develop a style manual for the client.

First, construct a detailed list of style items specific to the client. This list would include such things as the proper spelling of the client's name, abbreviations, titles, acronyms and the like. Most style inconsistencies occur in these areas. Unless you identify these areas clearly, you can't do a good job of recommending an appropriate client style manual.

Second, carefully study Example 6:1. This piece, written by Thomas W. Lippman, former editor of the National Weekly Edition of *The Washington Post*, explains to readers the tedious, sometimes contentious, issues confronted by a medium when it tries to write a new style manual.

Third, get a copy of the AP print and broadcast style manuals. Study carefully the contents of each section. Note what does not meet your client's needs.

Select one of the style manual types described in the second paragraph above. Submit a style manual to the client (your instructor). It should be a typewritten or word-processed report that shows detailed style provisions that meet the client's needs.

Independent 6 : 1

The Chamber of Commerce in your hometown does not have a style manual. Construct one for it. Follow the instructions detailed above.

Notes

Quick-Study

Extract, Chapter 7, "Memos, Email and Letters, Reports and Proposals," *Public Relations Writing: Form & Style* 6e, Belmont, California: Wadsworth, 2001.

When you become a professional public relations writer, you'll probably find that you write more memos, emails and letters than anything else. Even beginning writers write many of them. And you'll probably be surprised at how many reports and proposals you're expected to complete.

Organizations use *memos* mostly internally. Some companies have their own memo forms (See Example 7.1) and good word processing programs have memo formats. You merely insert information in the right places. You must rely on your best judgment when memo forms are not used, but consult the heading style in *PRW6e*. Memos often have more visual cues than letters, such as numbered lists, indented sections and other formats.

One common writing trap for memos and E-mails is the failure to give enough context for content. Just because people work with you, don't assume they have the background needed to understand your message. Don't be afraid to explain background, especially when writing to some-one you don't know or who is in another department or another organiza-tion.

A memo generally falls into one of six types. They are *bulletin, essay, informative, action, summary* and *file*. Review their descriptions in *PRW6e*. Personalize your memos. Pay attention to how they are distributed. If they are to be mailed, you may want to adopt a tone different from that of a memo to be posted.

Review Example 7.3 in *PRW6e* to refresh yourself about things to do or not to do with *Emails*. Emails seem to invite immediate responses. Sometimes these responses seem to be off-the-top-of-the-head. That isn't good busi-ness. Think before you write. Yes, it is acceptable to be less formal than in a business letter and perhaps not as structured as a well-ordered memo, but casualness that gets in the way of understanding is self-defeating. Email seems to be used in place of many memos and letters, although the number of letters being handled by the Postal Service continues to rise.

Letters are used mostly for communication outside companies (See Example 7.2). They are *information, solicitation, promotion, transmittal, cover* and *response* letters. Review *PRW6e* for a description of each. They may have as many as six parts: *heading, salutation, body, close, signature* and *reference matter*. Letters are generally a little more formal in tone than memos and emails. The situation and the relationship between the writer and the addressee govern the tone.

Organizations use letters extensively for promotional purposes. A modest investment in a promotional letter may yield big returns. To be truly productive, promotional letters must interest receivers and be written clearly and simply. The more you expect of readers, the clearer you must be.

Response letters deserve special attention. They usually are written to react to an occurrence or to something written or said.

Private response letters are directed to individuals. Sometimes writers say things in *private* response letters that they would not say if they knew in advance their letters might be made public. If it is to the advantage of the recipients to make your letters known to others, expect that they will be. Follow this simple rule: Never put anything in a letter, even a private response letter, that you don't want to see on the front page of the newspaper or leading the evening television news.

Public response letters are intended for public consumption, often written to correct information or to provide a different perspective. They appear as "letters to the editor" in newspapers and magazines, and they are heard on radio and seen on television (sometimes with supered segments of what you have said). Whether private or public, write persuasively but choose your words carefully because their tone reflects both mood and character.

You'll likely be writing reports and proposals too. A *report* is simply a well-documented research paper that gives background material that explains a subject. A *proposal* is equally well documented, but it usually advocates a course of action. Both reports and proposals use footnotes, tables, charts and related materials, depending on the topic and situation. Recall how you prepared and wrote essays, themes and research papers and reports when you were in school. If you don't remember how to source and cite materials, get a good style manual and keep it handy.

Although reports and proposals have different purposes, they usually have some things in common. Enclose a *cover letter* with each report or proposal. Address it to the person or group who will read the document. A cover letter briefly summarizes the content of the report or proposal. Use a *letter of transmittal* when the report or proposal was assigned by a person or group other than the recipient. A letter of transmittal defines who made the assignment, tells why it was assigned, and explains how the task was performed. It may also include a brief summary.

The *front matter* of a report or proposal includes such things as a title page, table of contents, and so on—much like the pages that precede the first chapter in a book. A *synopsis* page precedes the first page of the body of the report. Such a page is sometimes called an *abstract*, but the preferred label in the business world is *executive summary*. It is usually just one page, never more than two. It summarizes the highlights of the report or proposal. It must be complete enough that someone won't have to read the whole document to know what it is about.

The *body* of the report or proposal has three major elements: *introduction*, *body* and *conclusions*. The introduction reviews the problem and how it was studied. A thesis statement or hypothesis *provides a context for the body*. Anything not related to the central idea should be excluded from the body. Conclusions must be derived logically from the material in the body. Recommendations can follow conclusions, when appropriate.

Reports and proposals generally include *references*. These document the sources used to explain information not known commonly by those who read and evaluate reports or proposals. Always use footnotes or endnotes. And remember to include a complete *bibliography* of all information surveyed, including information consulted but not used.

An *appendix* contains detailed information important to the report or proposal but whose insertion in the body would disrupt reading. If you are writing to or are in a specialized field, use as little jargon as possible in your document. Expect to rewrite your report or proposal several times before you write it right.

Exercises Exercises **Exercises** Exercises

GEI 7 : 1

A GEI scientist has suggested that the lab make a formal proposal to join in a cooperative research proposal to get a grant for genome mapping of wheat. GEI management tells ProCom to follow up on the idea, and you are asked to write a proposal that management can submit to the university. Write a cover letter to go with the proposal to the university. Also write a short memo to management that explains the strategic idea behind the proposal. Spell out clearly the benefits to the university if the research is funded. This memo is especially important to the members of the management team who will negotiate with Dr. Lott and other university leaders.

NATS 7 : 1

Realizing that many accident victims are even more seriously injured at the accident scene by amateurish efforts to administer first aid, you suggest that ProCom produce for NATS a first-aid booklet quite unlike other first-aid booklets. Your booklet will visually not only illustrate the right way to do things but also the wrong way. Not only is the wrong way clearly illustrated, but the booklet also shows the sometimes-dire consequences of the incorrect administering of first aid. Write a memo to ProCom management that summarizes your idea. After some discussions with you, ProCom management has floated the idea with NATS. NATS management likes it and has given its approval for a rough draft of a few pages for review. Because it was your idea, ProCom assigns you the task of writing the draft. As it is to be only part of a completed booklet, you elect to do a representative section on a topic like CPR, emergency treatment of shock or severe burns or another emergency procedure. Create no more than four pages for this section of the booklet, including illustrations. When this section is complete, write a cover letter to NATS about what you want to present in the rest of the booklet. To do this assignment well, you'll need to review first-aid procedures. Consult the library and the Internet.

NCCC 8 : 1

Although Dr. T.A. Lott, president of State University, severed ties with ProCom when the scholarship scandal broke regarding Ms. Melody Hanzout, the relationship resumed when Lott called George Schuss, president of NCCC, and suggested NCCC establish a child-care center on campus to serve the needs of students, staff and faculty. Schuss told Lott that NCCC considers only proposals approved first by its agency, ProCom. He further suggested to Lott that the university work with ProCom to develop a proposal for such a venture. That's when Lott returned to ProCom. A primary motive behind Lott's approach to NCCC was a growing recognition that State University was experiencing higher-than-normal absences from work among faculty and staff because of illnesses. Lott had seen stories in the trade press that some firms had noted lower absenteeism from sickness when they provided child-care facilities for their workers. Prior to such help, a mother or father, awakening to find a 3-year-old running a fever, would call in sick in order to stay home. The employees themselves were not sick, but their children were. Lott further noted that this also made employees feel guilty. Dependable child-care programs not only seemed to decrease absenteeism but also improved morale because workers felt good about themselves and their employers. Lott's analysis was that State University probably would benefit from greater productivity if its faculty and staff had easy access to first-class child care for their youngsters. Ensuing discussions with Lott led to the conclusion that the proposal should recommend that NCCC develop a pilot program on campus. If the venture proved successful, it could be a model to market similar NCCC programs on campuses nationwide. You are assigned to write the proposal from Lott to Schuss, as well as a cover letter.

Independent 7 : 1

Get a copy of the advertising rate card used by your university's newspaper. Also get a copy of the policies the newspaper uses in accepting and/or refusing advertising. Review these policies and the rate card. Write a proposal for a new (or revised) set of policies and rate card intended to make them clearer and more complete. Also write a cover letter to accompany your proposal.

Notes

Example 7:1

This example announces ProCom's new interoffice memo form to be used by all staff members. The form was adopted to lend consistency to the look of ProCom.

ProCom *A Full-Service Communication Agency* **MEMO**

1 Professional Plaza, Serene, USA 95959. Phone: 123 456.7890. Fax: 123 456.8901. Email: www.procom.com

To:	All Staff Members	**Date:**	(Today's date)
From:	Professor	**Subject:**	New memo form

Effective tomorrow, all staff members are expected to use this new memo form. You can get a supply from the storeroom today. ProCom is using this new form to help it project a more consistent look. It will match the mailing labels, letterhead and other printed information about our organization.

Following is a brief review about the uses of memos.

Memos generally are to be used only for messages internal to our organization. Seldom should you use the memo form to communicate outside our ranks.

Memos should be brief and to the point. Think about the persons you're writing to and what they know about the topic of your memo. If they know a lot, keep background information to a minimum. If they don't know much about the topic, be sure to give enough information for them to understand and take appropriate action, if needed.

   Memos usually have more visual cues than letters, such as bullets, numbered lists, indented sections, etc.

Use bold faced type only to emphasize one or two points, as in the first sentence of this memo. Avoid italics except when writing out the formal name of a book or other publications.

Example 7:2

This example announces ProCom's new letterhead to be used by all staff members. It was adopted to lend consistency to the look of ProCom.

ProCom *A Full-Service Communication Agency*

1 Professional Plaza, Serene, USA 95959. Phone: 123 456.7890. Fax: 123 456.8901. Email: www.procom.com

(Today's Date)

Ms. Kari M. Backe
Executive Vice President
ProCom
1 Professional Plaza
Serene, USA

Dear Kari:

This letter is being written on ProCom's new letterhead. It should be used for all external correspondence, starting tomorrow. Get your supply of the new letterhead from the storeroom.

The new letterhead and other new materials are intended to unify the look ProCom projects to its clients and friends. Please encourage all staff members to use the new materials properly.

A similar letter is being sent today to each ProCom staff member.

If you think it is needed, you might consider a brief staff training session in which you go over the basics of good business letters. Good letters may have as many as six parts: heading, salutation, body, close, signature and reference matter (if any). Use your judgment about the need for training.

Sincerely,

I. M. Professor
President

Quick-Study

8

Extract, Chapter 8, "Backgrounders and Position Papers,"
Public Relations Writing: Form & Style 6e, Belmont, California: Wadsworth, 2001.

Backgrounders and *position papers* are especially important documents in public relations, but beginning writers seldom appreciate their true values. Backgrounders provide common information bases on topics. Position papers provide rationales for planned or completed actions.

Backgrounders have many uses. They provide source material for writers preparing ad copy, speeches, news releases, annual reports, newsletters, magazines and the like. Backgrounders go to reporters, to media and to other interested parties. They also may give context to media kits. Company executives consult them extensively when they plan and execute programs.

The key to writing successful backgrounders is the quality of the research that supports them. Review Chapter 4 in *PRW6e*. The information you need for a backgrounder is probably available. Your job is to find it. Rarely is primary research needed. If it is, do it.

Don't try to write a backgrounder until you know enough about the assigned topic. Begin with a declarative sentence that describes the backgrounder and why it is important. Begin writing the body of the document only when this sentence is perfected. Your backgrounder stresses history, trends, events, people, legislative actions and like matters relevant to the topic. Your task is to provide objective background and context for understanding the current scene. Then describe the current scene thoroughly.

Backgrounders often end with a presentation of the implications or consequences of taking one direction or action over others. Keep your *opinions* to yourself. Avoid editorializing. Let facts speak for themselves. Document everything you write. Cite the source for every fact that is uncommon knowledge to your readers. You must be a good scholar to do good backgrounders.

The term *position paper* describes what it is. It says, "This is where we stand on this matter." And it provides a rationale for that position. Like backgrounders, position papers require research. If you have good, current backgrounders, your research is done. You simply review the relevant backgrounders before working out a position. If you find holes in the information, do more research.

Write a declarative sentence stating your position. If you can't immediately reduce the position to a simple sentence, keep trying. Avoid qualifying clauses and phrases. Keep it simple. Take a position only after weighing related facts and issues. Build your paper on selected facts. Remember that a position paper should not recite history in detail. Nor should it be burdened with too many facts, like long lists of numbers, names and the like. That kind of information is for backgrounders.

Focus on the most important facts supporting your point of view. Advocate your position strongly, but fairly. Use footnotes or endnotes to cite the sources on which your position is based, although these are rarely as extensive in position papers as in backgrounders. Don't ignore other positions. You'll gain more supporters if you show accurately other points of view. That's because many of your readers will be no more than neutral toward your position. Some will be opposed to it. Both groups are naturally skeptical. If you do not show opposing points of view, even your supporters may have second thoughts about the position you advocate.

Remember your audience. Position papers are seldom written to a single audience. They may be used with many audiences, which makes writing an acceptable position paper more difficult than a backgrounder. The latter deals with facts. The former deals with opinion. Opinions are always debatable. Facts are less so. A good bibliography is always helpful.

Position papers also have some special uses. One is that they can be used as the basis for writing an essay to be submitted for publication on the op-ed page of newspapers. In fact, position papers may be fit fodder for the op-ed, perhaps with nominal editing and rewriting. Another is that position papers also may be used extensively as sources of image ad copy and PSAs. Backgrounders may contribute to these special uses, too, but properly done position papers should fill the need.

Formats for each document vary. Backgrounders and position papers used internally often are simply typed and copied for limited distribution.

If used outside the company, they may be typeset and printed for a better look. They are often three-hole punched so they can go into binders from which older versions have been discarded. Both documents use charts, graphs and tables. Always put these materials close to the narrative to which they apply.

Exercises Exercises **Exercises** Exercises

GEI 8 : 1

Fritz A. Horst, Ph.D., a research scientist at GEI, has some professional background in paleontology. He leans heavily on the order-analytical method (review GEI 5:2) of research, unlike the rest of his GEI colleagues who embrace the cause-effect method. Horst is upset that the recent proposal on genome mapping of wheat will rely exclusively on the cause-effect method. Horst, through his network of friends, has access to some grains of wheat, barley, maize and oats, some estimated to be 50,000 or more years old. He wants to be included in the proposed research program.

Glen Kowan and Lowell Garrett are absolutely opposed to the idea, not because they aren't comfortable with the order-analytical method but because they fear that including Horst will make it appear to potential granting agencies that GEI and State University scientists are spreading themselves too thin and that they lack focus.

Kowan and Garrett held a conference with I.M. Professor earlier today. They asked that a writer from ProCom be assigned the task of writing a one- or two-page position paper that spells out why GEI will concentrate on cause-effect research efforts. Professor calls you into the office and assigns the task to you. Professor says that a draft should be ready by a week from today at which time you are to meet with Kowan and Garrett to review the content.

Kowan and Garrett are aware that this position paper may motivate Horst to leave GEI, but that's a risk they are willing to take, although they value Horst's expertise. They also believe that this position paper will reassure other GEI scientists, and it will sharpen the organization's strategy.

NATS 8 : 1

One of NAT's beliefs is that emergency medicine centers are clogged with people who should not be there. Some are there because they have headaches or backaches or similar ailments that they can't bring under control with aspirin or Tylenol™. And they don't want to wait to see their own physicians the next day. Others are there because of accidents that could have been easily prevented. For example, poisonous chemicals may be stored carelessly, so they are easily accessible to children. Or a boiling pot is left unattended while someone answers a phone call in the next room. A curious child pulls the pot off the stove and gets burned severely.

NATS wants to develop a program that will educate and sensitize people to the need to practice good home and driving safety as a way of reducing the demand on emergency medicine centers. Before launching such a campaign, NATS has asked ProCom to develop a position paper that clearly defines the NATS position. ProCom assigns this task to you.

You'll need to do a good bit of library research about the state of emergency medicine. One issue you must address is the problem of poor people who depend on emergency rooms for their total health care because they can't afford regular physicians. When you finish the position paper, send it and a cover letter to Arty Hart.

NCCC 8 : 1

Nearly every business must be concerned with anything that affects the "bottom line," but particularly so with employees. If employees are preoccupied with the cost and quality of the care their children receive while they (the parents) are at work, employees aren't as productive as they might be. Some companies now argue that it is in the interest of their bottom lines to provide on-site, employer-subsidized child care for their employees' children. Employees pay only a nominal share of the cost. Some companies even provide these services free.

George Schuss and Sully Trotter see this trend as one that can benefit NCCC. They want to sell companies on the idea of developmental child-care centers. Although child-care centers must tend to the physical needs of children, NCCC believes these centers also should have clearly focused developmental roles. That's a point of view business has not fully accepted.

Schuss and Trotter asked ProCom to prepare a well-researched position paper that defines the benefits of developmental child-care centers.

They'll use this position paper to develop a marketing program to companies nationwide, touting NCCC as a vendor capable of providing these services on site. ProCom assigns this task to you.

You'll need to do a good bit of research on developmental child care. When you write the position paper, relate your findings to the benefits that can accrue to companies that use this approach to child care. When you finish, provide a cover letter from ProCom to Schuss and Trotter.

Independent 8 : 1

Choose an issue that is currently of concern on your campus. Do a thorough backgrounder on it. Then consider what you think about the issue, and write a report that details your position. Write a cover letter for both documents, addressed to your professor.

Notes

Quick-Study

9

Extract, Chapter 9, "News Releases for Print Media,"
Public Relations Writing: Form & Style 6e, Belmont, California: Wadsworth, 2001.

Many *news releases* for print media aren't used because they have no genuine newsworthiness. The attitude of managers in the print media is that if you want to see a puff piece in print, buy an ad. You must know what constitutes news for the media. And you must know your company well enough to recognize news when you see it.

Releases fall into seven types. The *announcement* release, as its name indicates, is an announcement of something. When your organization gets a new CEO, for example, you'll write an announcement release. "*Created news*" releases are used when your organization does something to call attention to itself, like a group of employees who organize to build houses for the poor through the Habitat for Humanity program. That creates news. When things happen that can't be anticipated, such as a fire in the No. 2 Generator of your power plant, you'll do a *spot news* release about it. If something happens that affects your organization, you will probably do a *response* release. It may be that you need to correct misinformation or to provide a different perspective. *Feature* releases are appropriate for human-interest stories or ones with unique angles, although they are light on news value. When something happens that you'd like to keep quiet but can't, you'll write a "*bad-news*" release. If you're trying to get information into a special column, into letters to the editor or on the op ed page, you'll be dealing with *special matter* releases.

The lead sentence or paragraph of a news release must be short. And it should have a local angle, not only to catch the editor's eye but also to interest readers. Develop the second paragraph and body of the story with concise sentences and precise facts about the *who, what, when, where, how* and *why*. Often the *why* governs whether a story gets printed. It also influences the type of play your release gets.

You'll be more successful at writing news releases if you play the role of a reporter for the newspaper or magazine for which the release is intended. The difference is that you can create quotes to fit your release. Always clear these quotes with the persons being quoted.

News releases must be simple, clear and direct in style. The unfortunate fact is that the writing in most news releases generally does not match the simplicity media professionals produce daily. Simplify. And always consult and follow the AP stylebook. Some media have their own styles. Know these variations on the AP style, and use them.

Sometimes you'll give news tips to the media instead of writing news releases. Tune into cyberspace to see what editors are looking for. If you have something that fits, your tips provoke interest among editors, they may assign reporters to write the stories. You'll be asked to help them with facts, site visits, interviews and the like. Stories written by media reporters usually get printed.

The focus of news releases varies with each situation. Some merely state information. Others relate special events or explain responses to events. Still others contain real spot news or feature materials, or are reactions to bad news.

Some material won't work as a straight news release, yet it may be important enough to appear in other forms, as a good guest column or as a brief in a local column. Ask editors about this before you write, and then use a writing style adapted to the column. Or write the piece as a letter to the editor. Being alert to these outlets will get a lot more exposure for your company. Don't force material into a news release if it does not fit the format.

For any news release, confirm that facts, spelling and grammar are correct. Expect your releases to be edited. If they appear with only nominal changes, that's a good sign you're doing things right. If they're edited heavily, you aren't doing your job well. Compare what appears in print with what you sent. Learn how to correct your mistakes by noting what professional editors do with your copy. When releases don't appear, this probably means you don't understand what is news. Compare releases not used to ones that are. You can sharpen your sense of news values from such a study.

Photographs, line art or schematics or other matter or tables should also be sent with news releases if this art adds interest to or explains content. Always provide complete captions; include names and titles of all people shown. Sometimes photos or other art, such as charts, with captions are run as "wild art." Most editors search daily for art to dress up their pages.

Help them out. You'll want to review the Associated Press PhotoExpress service through which you can deliver for a fee PR photos to more than 1,000 newspapers simultaneously.

Some organizations post their news releases on their web sites. Others don't. Editors generally take a pretty dim view of this, so you can't depend on them to search for news unless it is to follow-up on a lead or to get additional information on some story.

Because many media won't run your releases for lack of interest or space, be selective about where you send them and to whom. Address releases to people by names and titles, and be sure you know these people. If the content of a news release is best suited for the business section, send it to the business editor. Send it to the person who writes the column if you want the information to appear as a brief. If you send the same release to competing media in the same market, you'll make enemies of both. Write separate releases, each crafted individually.

Some media prefer to have news releases fed directly into their electronic systems. It's your business to know that and what those systems are like. Tailor your format to those needs. Be sure your software is compatible with theirs. If that means you must use several different software programs, do it. Before you send any news release, test it against the checklist in Chapter 9 of *PRW6e*. If you answer no to any of those questions, correct the problem now so that you won't regret it later.

Exercises Exercises **Exercises** Exercises

GEI 9 : 1

Everett C. Wagonseller, one of the investors from Omega Venture Capital, yesterday resigned from the Omega group and demanded that he be reimbursed immediately by other Omega investors for the $2 million that he contributed to the venture capital advanced to GEI. Wagonseller had been interviewed the previous day by a reporter from the *Chicago Tribune* in which he sought points of view on the cloning of humans and the extent to which the work at GEI could lead to that. The story appeared yesterday and quoted Wagonseller extensively. He claims he did not understand fully the work of GEI and had no inkling that the research by the GEI staff could contribute to the cloning process. "I'm a devout, conservative Christian who believes that cloning of humans is against God's eternal laws." He also said that he's embarrassed to be associated with such an effort and that he's taking steps immediately to withdraw any affiliation with Omega and GEI.

Other Omega investors became aware of this only after reading the story yesterday. They are, of course, upset that Wagonseller blasted both Omega and GEI without first saying something privately to affected parties. They met late yesterday afternoon at Chicago's O'Hare airport and agreed to return Wagonseller's money. Kowan and Garrett also attended the meeting.

The group issued a statement in which they announced the return of Wagonseller's money and apologized for the misunderstanding. They also said that they have no agenda for GEI to do research that results in cloning humans. "We're simply providing operating capital to an exceptional group of scientists whose work will contribute significantly to new knowledge about life and, perhaps, may result in improving the standard of living and health for all of humankind. We think that is a worthwhile goal, and we invite all interested parties to participate in that grand search."

Kowan this morning conferred with Professor about issuing a news release about the group's work. Kowan wants to make these points: 1) The search for new knowledge is always worthwhile, even if its discovery appears inconsequential at the time. 2) Research at GEI is working in three areas right now: a) GEI scientists are working to complete the sequencing the DNA of Droso-Phila and C. Elegans. Many genes are remarkably similar to human genes. Completed sequences of these may lead to clues that will help fight human diseases. b) GEI scientists also are at work on the marriage of microchips and DNA. They use chips to speed the process of quickly identifying genetic variations in tissues. Comparing diseased and healthy tissues can lead to understanding the cause of diseases. c) Other GEI researchers are working on family trees in which they identify and study large families, often from genetically isolated communities, together with computer technology to identify genes involved in complex disorders such as diabetes and heart disease.

Kowan says he expects the research role of GEI to grow and as it does current research will be expanded and new areas will be added.

Professor assigns you to do this release. Do a draft. Make up quotes for Kowan as they seem to fit the flow of the story. Review the draft with Dr. Kowan late today. Have him verify the essential facts as well as the quotes you've made up for him. If he wants to change them, let him.

NATS 9 : 1

In Assignment 8:1, you did a position paper explaining that emergency room over crowding could be alleviated with some preventive measures. One idea is to prepare a "different" first aid brochure—one that shows the right and wrong way to help accident victims. Since then, NATS has approved the concept and you've finished the brochure. It is now in production and will be ready for distribution in about a week. NATS has asked ProCom to prepare a news release on the new brochure. Because you know the brochure's purposes and content better than anyone else at ProCom, the news release assignment is given to you. NATS wants a release each to the Associated Press (as this brochure is expected to be distributed nationally), the *Clarion* and the state medical and nursing association publications. Also do a release for the NATS newsletter.

NCCC 9 : 1

The position paper in Assignment 8:1 was used as the basis for an NCCC proposal to State University for a model developmental child-care center. A contract was completed after lengthy negotiations. Among others, the contract has these provisions:

1. NCCC will construct its own facility on land provided by the university in a 99-year lease at $1 annually. If NCCC builds its facility and begins operations on the campus, ownership of the structure reverts to State University if NCCC decides to abandon the program for any reason. Abandonment also breaks the lease.

2. Client priorities are:

    A. Children of graduate students will be given first priority. Although the university will underwrite 25 percent of the costs for all children of graduate students, it will underwrite 75 percent of the costs for children of graduate teaching or research assistants.

    B. Children of undergraduate students have second priority. The university will underwrite 10 percent of the costs for children of all undergraduate students, but undergraduate lab assistants are underwritten at 25 percent.

    C. Children of hourly and professional staff members get third priority, and the university will underwrite their costs by 10 percent. Children of full-time employees earning less than $20,000 annually will be underwritten at 25 percent.

D. Children of tenured faculty members get fourth priority, and the university underwrites their costs by 10 percent. Faculty members with the rank of instructor or assistant professor on the tenure-track will be underwritten at 25 percent.

E. Children of townspeople will get fifth priority. There is no subsidy for these clients.

3. NCCC will employ at least eight faculty members 0.5 full-time-equivalent (FTE) at the university child-care center. These faculty members are specialists in clinical psychology and child development. Their academic homes are in the Department of Psychology and the School of Education at State University. This arrangement frees substantial budgeted funds the university can then use to cover the costs of developmental child-care subsidies.

Ground breaking for the NCCC center is scheduled for Friday of next week. Construction begins the following Monday. The center will be fully operational by the beginning of the next academic year.

The university's public relations office would ordinarily do a news release on this project, but that office has agreed to let ProCom do the release for NCCC. State University's PR office has pledged full cooperation regarding background materials. However, it wants to see a draft of the release before it is distributed to the media.

Because you've worked closely with NCCC on other projects, ProCom assigns the writing of the news release to you. What is needed is a release each for the *Clarion*, the Associated Press (state wire), the university's alumni magazine and internal newsletter and NCCC's newsletter.

Independent 9 : 1

Get the results of the most recent national survey of the attitudes of new college students (first-year students) and corresponding information about students at your university. Gallup, Roper, Harris and other pollsters do these studies routinely for some clients. The information often finds its way into the mass media.

Search such sources as *The New York Times Index* and *Reader's Guide to Periodical Literature* and the Internet until you find the data you need. Go to a reference librarian if you run into trouble. For data at your own university, look first to the Office of Institutional Research. If there isn't an office with that or a similar title, inquire at the university's public relations office. Nearly every campus does research of this type. Study the two sets of data for similarities and differences. Do a news release for the student newspaper about the differences you find.

Notes

Quick-Study

Extract, Chapter 10, "News for Broadcasting,"
Public Relations Writing: Form & Style 6e, Belmont, California: Wadsworth, 2001.

Journalistic concerns for news values, factual accuracy, spelling and grammatical correctness apply as much to broadcast writing as to print. But sights and sounds drive broadcast writing. And special events generally, except for crises, have the sights and sounds that get the most broadcast coverage, especially television coverage. So pay special attention to events that can lead to air time.

Much of your success at broadcast writing will depend on how well you prepare fact sheets that broadcasters can use. Supply a brief news release in broadcast style, although it may not get used as sent. Send along the print version, which is usually much longer, as information. Improve coverage by providing a segment of video- or audiotape.

If broadcasters cover a story on site, anticipate their needs for electrical power, staging areas, props and the like. Do everything you can to make their coverage as easy and as successful as possible. Use your own equipment to shoot or record the same event. This tactic provides good backup if their equipment fails. You also have an instant record of what happened at the event, which may be especially important in crises, or in ongoing controversial stories. And remember to post someone in a central area to answer broadcasters' questions and to provide information on demand.

You can call a news conference when someone from the company needs to interact with the media, or to announce a major development. Prepare for these events by writing or assembling fact sheets, backgrounders and position papers. These materials go into media kits along with broadcast and print news releases (the latter are for information only). Always cover your news conference as though you are a working member of the press. That not only helps you to see what happens from the media's points of view, but it also lets you spot weaknesses in your preparation.

Broadcast writing style is conversational. It uses active voice extensively. Broadcast writing also has two audiences. One is the announcer or other person who reads the copy aloud. The other audience is listeners or viewers. The physical appearance of the copy helps announcers. The copy's structure helps listeners or viewers. Broadcast leads seldom contain all the news elements seen in print news releases.

If you provide a video news release (VNR), remember that most television stations prefer to get VNRs via satellite, and they want to be notified that these are coming. Notify them via phone or fax when to expect the feed.

If you provide tape, radio places premiums on actualities (human voices and natural sounds of events or situations), but television prizes video with sound. Attach complete scripts to all audio- and videotapes. A news release that coincides with the tapes also helps broadcast news editors as they prepare newscasts.

Broadcast news stories are rewritten several times daily. That's why most stations want more information than is in your audio- or videotapes and scripts. It helps them dig for a new angle to freshen a story already aired several times. This is especially important to remember when you're dealing with crisis situations. Feed new information via phone or Email to stations as quickly as you can verify its accuracy. Also, post it on your Web site immediately.

Talk-show appearances can't be scripted in the strictest sense. Your role is to provide biographical and background materials. Sometimes the host or a station staff member will provide a sample list of questions that may be discussed. This list speeds up and focuses your preparation of appropriate background materials. But sometimes you know only the general topic, so the material you write or assemble must be more extensive. In both cases, you must rehearse the person who will be interviewed. Play the role of interviewer and be a devil's advocate. Never let the interviewee get surprised by questions you didn't expect.

Exercises Exercises **Exercises** Exercises

All Scenarios and Independent 10 : 1

Do broadcast versions of the assignment described in 9:1. Do one for local television and one each for two different (your choice) radio stations in Serene. For the television release, turn in a production script that uses voiceover (VO) and film or video actualities. For radio, turn in a production script that uses VO and audio actualities. Be sure your scripts are clearly marked as to VO and actualities.

Notes

Quick-Study

11

Extract, Chapter 11, "Features for Print and Broadcasting,"
Public Relations Writing: Form & Style 6e, Belmont, California: Wadsworth, 2001.

Most of the features you write as a PR professional probably will be for trade or industry magazines, employee newsletters or company magazines. Most features about your organization in the mass media probably will be written by media staff people or by free-lancers. You'll simply support their writing efforts by making information available, setting up interviews, arranging for visits and the like. Nevertheless, there are several key issues regarding how to prepare for, write and present features, whether you're actually writing them or helping those who do.

You must know your organization thoroughly so that you can clearly identify what is news or feature material. One clue is that good feature material often has a strong element of human interest. Look for the unusual, the dramatic, the surprising. Personal profiles or experiences, especially if they have one of the preceding qualities, can make good features. The same can be said for "how to" ideas.

Once you've identified a feature topic, you next must try to "market" it. Evaluate the kinds of feature materials produced by the media you may want to contact. Select a relevant medium that uses materials like your idea. Because your feature idea is related to your organization, you need approval from management before you go to the medium with the idea. That may be difficult because management knows that a reporter or free-lancer, not the organization, may be in control of what is written.

When you get clearance on the idea, write a query letter to the appropriate editor by name and title, proposing the feature. Outline the gist of the feature and explain how it fits into the needs of the audience of that medium. Really, a query letter is nothing more than a sales letter. Tell the editor what benefit there is to the medium and its audience. If the editor "buys" your idea, a reporter will probably be assigned to research and write the story. If it is a magazine, the assignment will probably go to a free-lancer. In either case, your role will be to lead interference for the writer by providing background information and arranging for interviews, tours, demonstrations and the like. You'll work closely with the writer and will have many opportunities to make suggestions. If the feature is about a complex topic, volunteer to read the final draft for accuracy, but don't be offended if your offer is rebuffed, especially by reporters, because most of them avoid any suggestion that smells of prior restraint.

Evaluating potential feature topics primarily involves three concepts. The first is reader (listener, viewer) *interest*. If you judge it objectively as no more than moderately interesting, don't bother with getting management's OK and, above all, don't bother an editor with it. The second concept is reader (listener, viewer) *consequence*. Some ideas may not bubble with interest, but they may be important to audiences. Editors deal with content daily that is a blend of what an audience should have and what it wants. So a feature idea that is low in interest may be important enough for an editor to "buy." The last major concept is the idea of *angle or slant*. Really good features have a twist to them that grab and hold the attention of audiences. At the time you conceive a feature idea, it may come with a unique angle or slant. Most don't. It is usual that you develop an angle or slant after you're well into the research for the piece.

Research for features usually involves two basic steps. The first is to mine all pertinent *secondary research* information, especially from the Internet. That means lots of time in the library sifting computer-search output for appropriate background information. The final phase of this step is to organize what you've learned about the topic. Be especially sensitive to gaps in your information so that you can go back and fill them. The second major step is *to interview* authoritative people about the topic. As your interviews progress, be sensitive to new pieces of information that amplify what you have found or to ideas that seem to contradict what your earlier research had suggested. You may develop an angle or slant during the secondary research phase, but make sure that what you learn in interviews reinforces that approach. More often than not a good angle or slant will emerge during your interviews, especially if you remain alert.

Keep in mind several key issues as you write a feature. Some people say the most important part of a feature is its first sentence, or lead. Their thesis is that if you don't immediately grab the attention of an audience, you can't expect the audience to go deeper into the story. Good point. So work hard at developing a good lead. If you have a good angle or slant, writing a good lead is much easier.

Develop the body of the feature so that it flows naturally from the lead. The body also has to verify (reinforce) the idea of the lead and to illustrate and amplify it. Facts, statistics and the like should be reserved for this part of the story, but go as light as possible on numbers. Remember to describe things with simple words and phrases. Analogies often help, especially if the topic is complex. Anecdotes generate audience involvement. It gives them things to identify with. Use quotations, but not too extensively. Quotes not only explain and reinforce the point of the lead, they also humanize the story. Be sure to put drama in the story, but don't overdo it to the point it becomes unbelievable. If you work these elements into your story, it probably will be a good one.

If you're doing a feature for radio or television, there are additional points to observe. A feature for radio or television probably will be in the range of three to four minutes; this is called a *minidoc*. It is researched like any other story, written in broadcast style, then broken into stand-alone segments for serial broadcasts. Remember to do these features as if you are on the staff of the station. Provide a full script with each audio- or video-tape you send to stations. If there is a print version of the same story, send it along, too. Features can also be documentaries of 20 to 60 minutes. These are usually produced in cooperation with a particular television station. Radio stations seldom use long features.

Exercises Exercises **Exercises** Exercises

GEI 11 : 1

Review what you did in GEI 9:1 and 10:1. The blast from Wagonseller set in motion a meeting of Omega investors and Kowan and Garrett the next day. The group issued a statement. The following day you did print and broadcast releases for GEI. What Professor has asked you to do now is to do a print feature story (a broadcast version may be needed later) that focuses on the potential benefits of the complete sequencing of Droso-Phila and C. Elegans, the two organisms that GEI scientists are working on now.

Interview some of the scientists who are involved in this project now. Make up their names and titles and their quotes. It also is a good idea to interview some of the biology faculty at your university to get first-person perspectives about what this work is all about and its potential applications. You'll want to spend some time in the library also and mine the Internet for current information about gene research.

The hope is that if GEI can complete the sequencing of DNA in Droso-Phila and C. Elegans, this may lead to some significant breakthroughs in the fight against a wide range of diseases. If so, improved treatments and new drugs may be highly profitable to GEI. And this work might improve the quality of life for a wide range of people.

Improving the quality of life of people, not profits to GEI, is the angle that Professor has suggested that you work on. That gives you a great deal of room in which to maneuver. Because of Dolly, the Dorset sheep, be sensitive to the fact that many people, even if it is unstated, fear that cloning is the hidden agenda of many genetic researchers. Some even see it as an inevitable outcome. That would present an enormous strain on society because cloning humans would become ethical, religious, philosophical and legal flash-points.

It is GEI's hope that your feature can build a convincing argument about the value to society of DNA research. That's a large hope and it is unrealistic to think that one feature will turn people around, but it can help. So, don't try to change the world with your writing but stake out a small area on which to focus your efforts.

NATS 11 : 1

Refer to what you did in Assignments 8:1, 9:1 and 10:1. NATS will be ready in three months to begin distribution of about 1 million copies of its first aid brochure. The brochure not only explains in detail how to give proper first aid but also emphasizes what not to do. It is believed that the latter point is what will make the NATS brochure more useful to people who have little or no prior training in giving first aid. NATS hopes to break a major feature story in a significant magazine just prior to the beginning of distribution. Because the brochure deals with such serious matters, the NATS leadership, especially Sally Forth, wonders if a light, humorous feature might be the best way to introduce it to the intended audience: people who have little or no training in giving emergency first aid. Forth phones and discusses that idea with Professor at ProCom.

Professor says that one of the ProCom staff will handle the assignment. But Professor is careful to say to Forth that this will take some boning up, not just reviewing the contents of the booklet, on some humorous things that have happened to people being given first aid or to those giving it. Anecdotes must be chosen with care, otherwise the story might turn off readers in a hurry; editors might then shun the story. Forth agrees, so Professor passes the assignment to you. Professor wants the first draft of the feature by a week from today.

NCCC 11 : 1

As you know from Assignments 9:1 and 10:1, construction of a new child-care center by NCCC on the State University campus is under way. It is scheduled for operation August 15, just in time for the next academic year. Although ProCom has already done news releases on the ground breaking and early construction, its staff has taken on a variety of other tasks, such as writing a promotional brochure, videotape and several items for a media kit to be ready at the time of the formal opening.

One of the tasks as yet unassigned is to do a magazine feature on the concept behind the center. Professor assigns you that task. You are to identify an appropriate magazine and do a query, accompanied by a proposed writing outline, to the editor. Assume that the editor "buys" your idea and promises to run the feature if it meets the magazine's exacting standards for excellence in writing and critical thinking. It is now time for you to do the magazine feature.

Refer to information you prepared for NCCC as its proposal to State University. Supplement this material with information from the library about early childhood development. As you prepare to write, keep alert to a particular angle or slant that will set your feature apart from ordinary features on child development. Professor has suggested that you look for angles related to the concept of development as compared simply to child care. Professor wants a first draft of this piece within 10 days. You can create quotes from appropriate people at NCCC and State University, but be sure to clear the quotes with them before the feature is given to the magazine.

Independent 11 : 1

Events like date rapes, parental divorces or lovers' quarrels, among many others, are traumatic experiences for anyone who endures them. Some people handle these emotional disruptions better than others—at least outwardly. But most people can benefit by having a third party with whom to share these experiences. That's why crisis centers are staffed around the clock to help people in distress. Some people who contact the centers need only to "unload" on someone. Others may be in need of professional counseling or other help. Crisis centers can help direct them to the proper places. Plan and write a story about crisis centers.

Do some background reading in the library. Select a magazine that might be interested in your feature. Obviously, *Sports Illustrated* is not a likely choice, so exercise some care in making your selection. Review several editions of the magazine, noting the angles used in stories, the style of writing and related matters. If there's no crisis center in your area, change your focus to shelters for battered women. Make contact with the center's director, and arrange for an interview. Do the interview and any subsequent research needed after the interview. Work out an angle for the story, and then write a feature for the magazine you selected.

Notes

Quick-Study

Extract, Chapter 12, "Message Design Concepts,"
Public Relations Writing: Form & Style 6e, Belmont, California: Wadsworth, 2001.

Because all public relations messages seek to persuade target publics, it is a good idea to review the persuasive message designs described in Chapter 3 of *PRW6e*. Good message designs not only stem from appropriate persuasive strategies, they also involve the careful integration of words, images, motion and sounds into messages that easily and clearly convey ideas to relevant publics. The most successful ones are often notable for their overall simplicity. A casual review of messages in today's media and the Internet seems to suggest that too many people don't understand that point very well. That is why this chapter is devoted to some broad concepts that you can use as you write and design messages of all types.

All messages begin with a simple process. You must gather relevant information and analyze it in light of the needs of your client and target publics. This analysis should suggest several creative strategies. You'll evaluate these and select the one you believe is best. Then you'll focus on tactical applications. This is where you begin to make choices about words, visuals, sounds, type, color, and so on to give form and substance to the message.

Concentrate on the clarity of the message you are designing. If you're using several media to send it, pay particular attention to the consistency of what is said and shown in these tactical variations. Clarity and consistency are paramount to building a good message and campaign. Remember that the verbal part of the message should control the selection and use of all elements in the message. Using as few elements as possible tends to add clarity and consistency. Always remember to simplify everything. The message need not be simpleminded, just clear and consistent with all others.

Even when you have a good creative strategy, good tactical interpretations are often difficult to execute. That's because you must use a variety of symbols to represent what you want to convey. Symbols are not real. They only represent ideas or things. And that explains why some people may interpret your message in ways you don't intend. You are a writer, of course, and words are the most common symbols you deal with daily. If you remember to concentrate on concrete words, target publics are less likely to misinterpret what you say than if you rely mostly on abstract words. Be explicit. Shun implications.

Strive for good organization of your message. It should flow from point to point and lead target publics naturally through the message. The way you write the message helps with the organization. And the way it is laid out in printed form or presented on television or computer screens also gives a sense of organization. Layout is the physical arrangement of all elements in the message. Even if target publics are not skilled in the nuances of presentation, haphazard organization may prompt people to wonder if they should volunteer their attention. Many don't.

When you're satisfied with the verbal part of the message, begin thinking of visuals that might convey the message clearly. Art of all kinds should offer a visual version of the verbal message and reinforce it. It isn't enough for visuals to be pretty, provocative or exciting. They must communicate or they should not be used.

Several points should be kept in mind as you deal with the overall message design. People tend to perceive a message by grouping information by similarity, proximity and continuity. Elements that don't fit arouse dissonance. This may prompt questions about the message itself as well as its source, and that may drive away target publics. People also tend to "see" things that are not explicit in messages. This invites misinterpretations and unintended consequences. Remember that clarity and consistency tend to be explicit, not implicit. When target publics see your message, they filter it through their individual past experiences. They apply their own values and belief systems to interpret the meaning of your message. You can't control their interpretations. You only can strive for clarity and consistency that tend to minimize different interpretations.

Keep these perceptual processes in mind when trying to understand some major visual principles: Balance (formal and informal, including visual weight), horizontal and vertical lines, contrast, movement, harmony, unity and proportion. Study these in detail and keep in mind that color is an important part of effective message design. We encounter color everywhere. It may depress us or make us feel happy. It may suggest springtime freshness or, like some odors, drive us away from something. Hence, it is important that you understand the emotional, psychological impact of color.

We've repeatedly emphasized consistency of look in messages. One way to build in consistency is to use a logo. A good logo makes a positive impression. It is also unique so that it isn't confused with competitors and it is durable. Probably the most important aspect of good logo is that it must work equally well across all media.

When you've worked out what you think is a good verbal content, think about how you will make it visible in your message. Type is the way words are made visible. Not just any type. Type has qualitative, connotative dimensions just as it has physical dimensions. Good verbal content can suffer dramatically by poor type selection. Experiment with different fonts to see how compatible they are with what you're trying to convey. You want to choose the type carefully. Digital systems now make it possible to modify type into a piece of art, just like photographs and drawn art.

If the message you're working on is complex, the use of infographics may help to clarify it. These devices include charts (bar, column and pie) diagrams (including cutaways), organizational charts (that shows lines of authority), systems flow charts (that show sequential movement), maps and bulleted or numbered lists. But don't use them just because you can.

A message for radio or other audio can be, if done well, the most creative of all media because it is staged in the theater of the mind. That's a vast territory that many people get lost in. Good message design here places priority on writing that is precise, concise and evocative. Words must be chosen not only for their exact meaning but also for their emotional impact. Sound effects used strategically can amplify these words so people can "see" the message in their heads. When the design is done well, no other medium can be more persuasive than radio or audio.

Message designs for television, video, film and the Internet are much more restrictive than radio or other audio. That's because images on the screen tend to tunnelize people's perceptions of what they are seeing. Images that don't match the words can be disastrous. Try to maximize a major asset of these media—the ability to show movement. Movement attracts attention, but it can hold it only if the verbal content and images blend well.

All Scenarios and Independent 12 . 1

Search for a message (brochure, catalog page, ad, etc.) that you believe does not have a good overall message design. Find another that you believe is very good. Remember that message design as used here refers to all copy, visuals, color, type and other physical elements in the message, including the layout. Compare and analyze these two messages for their good and bad qualities. For example, do the images say the same thing visually as the verbal content? How well is the message organized? Does the message flow logically and lead people naturally through its content? Does the color, if used, seem to be psychologically appropriate to the verbal content? These are only starter questions. Review Chapter 12 before you do this exercise. Make a list of questions or issues you should address in the comparison and analysis. Submit your report of no more than three pages, typed double spaced or word processed. Attach the items you've chosen to compare and analyze.

Notes

Quick-Study

13

Extract, Chapter 13, "Writing Advertising Copy,"
Public Relations Writing: Form & Style 6e, Belmont, California: Wadsworth, 2001.

Y ou'll write a lot of advertising copy, but rarely for commercial products or services. Your efforts will focus on "idea" ads, sometimes called *advertorials*, if for print media, or *infomercials*, if for broadcast. You'll also write some *institutional, identity* or *corporate image* ads. But you'll write more *PSAs* than any other type of ad. PSA stands for a *public service ad* in print or a *public service announcement* in broadcast. The media run PSAs free as a public service on a space- or time-available basis.

Advertising copy is persuasive. It asks people to accept an idea, take a position, buy a product or use a service. Advertising appeals are vital to effective persuasion. Appeals may be *rational, emotional* or a *combination* of the two. Rational appeals tug at the head, and emotional appeals tug at the heart. Combination appeals begin with emotion to arouse attention and interest, switch in the body of the copy to a rational approach intended to provide reason-why information and end with a final appeal to the heart.

Appeals are also important when positioning your point of view. A road bond program positioned as a "safety" issue may get more support than if positioned merely as a "better roads" issue. An audience pays attention and responds positively to your messages for its own reasons, not yours. If the appeal you select is unimportant to your audience, your ads will be ineffective.

Basic guidelines for writing advertising copy include:

1. Know the purpose of your ad.
2. Know the objective facts about the topic.
3. Know what is important to your audience. If what you want is unimportant to your audience, reconcile the differences.

4. Know which media your audience pays attention to, and package your message in the right formats for those media.

5. Be original and creative in how you tell your story. Avoid triteness, mundaneness, cuteness and cleverness.

6. Think verbally and visually as you write. Use vivid words, and illustrate them with evocative art, scenes, motion and/or sounds.

7. Use simple words, phrases and grammatical structures.

8. Repeat the central idea at least three times in each message, although it need not be repeated verbatim.

9. Expect to repeat the message several times before a threshold of effects (enough exposures to a message for it to begin to register with the receiver) is reached.

Decide whether your primary purpose is to *inform* or *persuade*. If it is to inform, your copy probably will be information-intensive. If it is to persuade, you'll use less information, but select it carefully to support your point of view.

Good copywriting follows four basic steps. Although these steps are most easily recognized in print messages, they apply equally to broadcast and film.

1. Getting an audience's *attention* is the first step. Provocative headlines and visuals can achieve this goal. Headlines that promise a benefit get the most attention.

2. *Interest* is piqued by the headline and the first sentence or paragraph of the copy by appealing to the audience's self-interest. Only if self-interest is aroused can you transfer it to interest in what you advocate.

3. The body of the copy should heighten *desire* for and *credibility* in what you advocate by supporting claims made or benefits promised. It establishes associations between facts and ideas about them.

4. The final step is to invite *action*. Effective ads always call for specific action, such as to support the United Way, to volunteer with the local literacy program or a myriad of others.

Simple words, phrases and grammatical structures are also hallmarks of good ad copy.

These same principles apply to writing copy for direct mail, mail-order and unmailed direct advertising and to all sales promotion materials. Creating effective outdoor ads may be the sternest measure of your skills as a copywriter. For an outdoor ad, you can't use more than about eight words of copy, including the client's name. You will find that especially challenging. Use that same guideline for banner ads on the Web. Some ads on the Internet are integrated into the format of a program so they appear to be seamless. For these, observe the guidelines outlined in *PRW6e* for television, but you may find program content somewhat restrictive.

Preciseness, conciseness and clear style are hallmarks of broadcast and film copywriting. Such copywriting must be simple, direct and provocative. It should be conversational in tone so that it sounds personal. Avoid generalities, exaggerations, slang and jargon.

A slice-of-life (SOL) technique is often favored because it easily portrays problems audiences can identify with and offers solutions. Jingles and humor are usually highly memorable. However, both can grow stale quickly. Heavy-handed humor can backfire. If you use humor, never poke fun at your audience.

Exercises Exercises **Exercises** Exercises

GEI 13 : 1

Some time ago, GEI's management team reviewed your position paper about why the lab will concentrate on using cause-effects research methods. The team was so impressed with the way you pulled the position paper together in Assignment 9:1 that it has asked ProCom to assign you to develop a public service campaign that promotes the recognition and appreciation of this method of research and how it may lead to important discoveries. Some of these discoveries may result in improved domestic plants and animals that yield a more dependable food supply. Others may lead to new medicines, treatments or cures for a range of human diseases. The purpose is not to promote GEI but to promote the benefits of this method of research used by thousands of scientists around the world. The GEI advisory board has also endorsed this idea.

Your instructions from Professor include:

1. Write a basic communications strategy for the campaign.
2. Write a basic creative strategy for the campaign's messages.

Although you'll do six or eight for the campaign, ProCom wants you to do only three versions, one each for newspaper, radio and television. ProCom's creative team will review the two strategy statements and your model messages before they're shown to the principals at GEI.

NATS 13 : 1

A continuing problem for NATS members is too much demand in many emergency rooms, especially in metropolitan areas. This demand leads to long hours for physicians and other staff people. It is aggravated by people who want emergency care when they really don't need it or they need care because they have not practiced good driving or home safety measures. These cases not only tax emergency care personnel, but they also deny proper care, in some cases, to those who need it most.

The position paper you prepared for NATS on preventable accidents has been reviewed carefully. The NATS leadership is now prepared to commit to an extensive, persuasive communication program intended to sensitize people to the problems of emergency medical care.

The program's basic purpose is to lighten the pressure on emergency care centers by helping people understand how to prevent the need for emergency care. Because of the quality of the position paper you did, NATS has requested that ProCom assign you this task. ProCom has agreed.

The first task you're assigned is to develop a communications strategy for the overall program. The next step is to develop a creative strategy that will focus the campaign. NATS wants to see newspaper, television and radio versions of a sample PSA before it gives full approval to the program.

NCCC 13 : 1

The NCCC leadership is excited about the early success of the child development center on the State University campus. Part of the excitement is because NCCC sees itself as contributing significantly to the education of students in the university's child development programs. It also feels that it is providing a living laboratory for faculty members, who can conduct their research on site.

Response from graduate students and faculty has been exceptionally good. They feel their children are being handled well by NCCC. Staff members report that children at the center are far better than average in terms of innate intelligence, and most are developmentally from six months to more than two years ahead of their chronological ages. This finding has presented some significant new challenges to the NCCC staff, who appear to thrive on challenges.

NCCC management believes it is time to "go public" with some image ads in a few prestigious journals and a "canned" one-time program for use on public television. NCCC has asked ProCom to assign you these tasks because of the excellent position paper you wrote in Assignment 9:1. But before NCCC authorizes the full program, it wants to see one sample print ad and a few pages of a proposed television script.

Independent 13 : 1

Write one each of a television and radio spot to be run locally. The focus of these spots is to promote the campus newspaper as a good place for certain types of businesses to advertise. You'll need to get as much information as possible about the local campus market and the readership of the campus newspaper. Be sure you understand the nature of buying behaviors and preferences of students at your University. Don't confuse them with the buying behaviors and preferences of faculty and staff.

Notes

Quick-Study

14

Extract, Chapter 14, "Writing for Web Sites,"
Public Relations Writing: Form & Style 6e, Belmont, California: Wadsworth, 2001.

Use of the Internet seems to be growing exponentially. As a public relations writer you frequently will use the *World Wide Web* for research. This exposes you to a variety of Web sites. The *home page* is the first screen you see when you call up a site. Because we now have more experience with sites and their design, the Web looks better than it did just two or three years ago. But there still are too many sites that are not as useful or as inviting as they should be.

It isn't likely that you'll be assigned the task of building a Web site, but you may be asked to draft some or all of its content. You need not be an expert at site building, but there are a few basic concepts that you need to understand before you try to write anything. To get on to the Web, you must use a *Universal Resources Locator* (URL). This is the site's name. When you enter a URL, a browser searches out the server that handles that URL and connects you to it. The first screen that comes up on your computer is called the home page. That label does not refer to all the pages on a site but only to the first page. It usually contains some sort of directory with buttons to click to help you find the information you want. This is called *navigation*.

The content of Web sites may change often, depending on the nature of the organization or individual the site represents. Visitors to sites usually are seeking specific information. Because of that, most visitors don't read information word for word. They skim, scan and jump around until they find what they want. This behavior is opposite of reading behavior in other media. It also influences the way you must write. However, good Web writing is like writing for other media in that you must be concerned first with strategy and then with tactics. Strategy deals with what you want to say. Tactics deal with how you say and show it. It is at this tactical level that Web writing generally is much different from other kinds of writing. Good grammar, proper punctuation and correct spelling apply to Web writing, of course, but a casual review of some sites seems to suggest that many prople don't abide by those criteria. You should also minimize the use of adjectives and adverbs because they may fatten your writing unnecessarily.

Even if you write beautifully, the reading behavior of visitors demands that you organize your writing for quick, easy scanning. Visitors seem to gravitate to headlines, subheads, words and links that you emphasize in some way. You'll improve your writing if you first develop a flow chart that positions content in some logical order. Be careful not to bury a major part deep inside copy. Put it in a headline, subhead or, at least, in a short, pithy sentence at the beginning of a copy block. Sites also are somewhat like memos because they use lots of numbered or bulleted lists. These devices help visitors locate information quickly. You'll need to build in appropriate links to other parts of your site as well as to other sites. The objective is to make it as easy as possible for visitors to get the information they want. Remember that long copy is much harder to read on the screen than it is on a printed page, so keep it brief.

You may be called on to serve as liaison with a site builder. If so, there are a few issues with which you should be familiar. The idea of simplification not only applies to your writing, but also to the site's physical appearance and organization on the screen. Insist on a screen that is not cluttered. Limit the number of visuals on the screen and keep them small. If it takes more than 20 seconds to download a screen, many people will exit your site and go elsewhere. Insist on information-filled heads and subheads. Visitors find these to be useful qualities. Group related screens in a logical order. Each screen should be free-standing so visitors don't have to scroll up and down. There should be a consistent look from one screen to the next. Insist on appropriate links. Don't link just because you can. Do it with purpose and relevance. Be sure to build in a home page link on every screen so visitors won't have to navigate back through previous pages to find home.

Graphics on a Web site are no less important than they are in other media. One issue is the selection of type fonts and sizes. Concentrate on *readability* and *appropriateness*. It is suggested that type size for copy be no less than 12 points. Line lengths should be about twice the length in picas as the point size of type, plus or minus up to three picas. Many computer systems now can reproduce millions of colors. But most people can only see a small fraction of these variations and most printers can't reproduce all of them. Limit the system to 256 colors, the minimum for most systems. Background color should be in a very light gray or in white or egg-shell tones. Visuals should be kept small to enhance downloading for visitors. If a big visual is needed, use a thumbnail on the screen and give visitors the option of downloading a larger version if they want it.

Think of the construction of a Web site as an exercise in branding. A site map helps visitors to navigate through your site more readily. A good site also provides the means for visitors to respond with questions, comments, orders and so on. You should also look carefully at ways to track usage. This is especially important when revising the site to make it more useful. You also should also work out a schedule for refreshing your site.

Exercises Exercises **Exercises** Exercises

All Scenarios and Independent 14 : 1

Review what you did in Exercises 8.1, 9.1, 10.1, 11.1, 12.1 and 13.1. This review will help as you begin to think critically about what ProCom's I. M. Professor is assigning you now. The client has asked Professor to develop a plan for a Web site. After discussing this need in detail with the client, Professor has assigned you the task of developing an overall plan for the client, consisting of two parts. Professor wants you to write a rationale for the site and submit with it a flow chart that shows the categories of information you believe should be included.

The rationale should explain in detail why the site is needed. It also should summarize the benefits to the client and who might visit the site for what purpose, among other things. It might be helpful to review the General Motors site map in Example 14.2 in PRW6e. A site map is not a flow chart, but it does illustrate broad categories of information. A flow chart includes similar broad categories. The difference is that each broad category has subcategories of information much like a writing outline. Its purpose is to serve as a guide for how information on the site will be organized. Also, think in terms of links within the site as well as possible links to other sites on the World Wide Web.

You may use a writing outline format if you're more comfortable with that rather than a flow chart. The rationale should be no longer than two pages, typed or word processed double spaced. The flow chart or outline should be attached.

Notes

Quick-Study

Extract, Chapter 15, "Campaign Writing and Media Kits,"
Public Relations Writing: Form & Style 6e, Belmont, California: Wadsworth, 2001.

A communication campaign plan defines *what* is to be done, *how* it will be done, *who* will do it, *when* it will be done and *how often* it will be done. Development of a campaign includes first a review of the organization's mission. Relevant information is gathered and analyzed, and forecasts are made. These lead to the setting of objectives and goals, which, in turn, shape organizational strategy. Message and media strategies are refined, methods of control are agreed to and provisions for coordination are worked out. At that point, tactical policies, processes and techniques begin to unfold and are applied. The final part of a campaign is monitoring its progress and evaluating its effectiveness.

The role of the writer usually is focused on the area of message strategy and the creation of relevant messages for the campaign. But the entire plan must be studied carefully to make sure the writer's role is perfectly clear. Three major reasons make this so:

1. Each message in a campaign must be consistent with all others.
2. Each message must be tailored specifically for a particular audience.
3. Each message must be written to fit the format of the medium used to deliver it.

It should be obvious that the writer must understand clearly the mission of the organization. That is necessary to make sense of the data in the situational analysis and to see its relevance, especially as it pertains to target publics. The forecasts are, of course, educated guesses of what can or will happen in the future. And the writer needs to know how these forecasts may affect the writing portion of the campaign. Without this background, the objectives and goals of the campaign may make little sense, because these are supposed to define what is expected of the campaign. Organizational strategic decisions that indicate incremental steps to be taken are critical to the writer. That is because message and media strategies must be derived from them. The flow and development must be clear, logical and sequential.

Writers must keep in mind several key concepts regarding message strategy. *Simplicity* is one of the key elements. Strategy that is complex usually proves to be less effective than was hoped. Keep it simple. A good creative idea is not only simple but also *adaptable*. It must work equally well in a variety of contexts and in any combination of media. It must be easily *applicable* to every message, in whatever form, in the campaign. And a good message strategy is *durable*. It has staying power that can carry a campaign over long periods of time.

Good media strategy has certain features. It seeks to identify the media a target public pays most *attention* to. It considers the relative *credibility* of various media. Some media impart more credibility than others in the eyes of a target public and, therefore, have rub-off value that may increase the believability of what the PR writer says. *Timing* is an important consideration. Some messages must be delivered within a very narrow time frame. Timing may have little value in other situations. Good media strategy also places high value on *effective reach*. That means that a medium will be selected because it reaches a high percentage of the target public, not just because it has impressive gross circulation or audience numbers.

The PR writer must be careful to make sure that what is written fits within the central strategic thrust of the campaign. That's what makes the visible parts of a campaign a campaign. What the target public sees is a series of "connected" messages over time in a variety of media.

One of the most difficult assignments for a PR writer is to take the evaluation of a campaign and break it down into simple messages aimed at different groups within an organization. Although this can be difficult, it is also one of the most important assignments given to a PR writer, and it usually calls for a high level of persuasive skill.

Use the term *media kit* rather than *press kit*. Picky? No, because PR professionals prepare packages, or kits, of information for all the media, not just for newspapers or the "press." Contents vary, based on their intended use. They usually are prepared with particular media involved; that is, one kit is prepared for newspapers and magazines, another kit for radio and still another for television. You'll need extra copies on hand, however, so that you can respond to special requests for additional information. For example, television reporters might want a copy of the print media kit because it may have more in-depth information in it. Or they might want a radio kit because they want easy access to audio tapes, segments of which might be integrated into the visuals they shoot.

The shell of a media kit is simply a basic folder, usually with pockets inside, printed with the organization's name, address and/or logo on the front. These serve well, but you may want to create a unique shell if you're doing a significant special event. All media kits must contain a letter to the person who will be using the information. This letter often focuses on a description of the materials found in the kit. It is intended to make it easier for users to quickly recognize and extract the information they want. If kits are mailed, the letter should be a cover letter attached to the front of the shell. In every case include names and phone numbers of people to contact for clarification or additional information.

Media kits are used to give basic information about an organization, special events (preliminary and on-site), news conferences and crises. Remember that media kits are intended for the hands-on use of working members of the news media. Basic content includes:

1. A *facts sheet* about the organization, including items such as names, addresses and phone numbers of officers and a description of what the organization is, makes or does;

2. A *historical facts sheet* that focuses on the organization's founding and development, especially important milestones;

3. *Biographical information* on the leadership of the organization with pictures (head shots)—8-by-10-inch black and white glossies for the print media and 3-by-5-inch (matte finish) for use as identification by broadcasters;

4. A *backgrounder* that explains the nature of the organization and what it does;

5. *Position papers* on relevant topics that explain the organization's stance;

6. Editions of an organization's *magazine(s)* or *newsletter(s)*, especially issues whose content may bear on the situation that calls for the current media kit; and

7. A page or two of *selected facts*, each of which can stand alone and is interesting, about the organization. If your organization has an *annual report*, put it in the kit also, along with any *informational brochures* on hand.

Doing media kits on CD-ROMs is now common with some organizations. You can pack a lot more information into a CD-ROM and you can use color, sound and motion. Consult Chapter 15 in *PRW6e* for guidelines to be used for different kinds of media kits.

Exercises Exercises **Exercises** Exercises

All Scenarios 15 : 1

The phone rings and a secretary tells you that I. M. Professor wants to see you now. You save and close the computer file you're working on, pick up a note pad and a pencil and head for Professor's office, all the while wondering what's up. Professor greets you with a smile, which is a little alarming because Professor has never smiled much at you. You're invited to sit down, and Professor offers you a cup of hot spiced tea, which you take somewhat cautiously because you detest hot tea. Professor talks about the weather, opera and other things. All the while you're becoming more alarmed. "Why on earth am I here?" you wonder. Finally, Professor gives you a measured look and says, "I got a call from your client about two hours ago." You nod, thinking that maybe the client was complaining about some job you'd done. "I've been talking with them about their need for a fully developed communication plan, and they've finally given me the go-ahead," Professor said. "The interesting thing," says Professor, "is that the client has asked me to assign you to the project." You're surprised but pleased.

Then Professor describes how to approach the task. Review everything known about the client. Begin with its mission and move forward. Write a skeleton communication plan. By skeleton, Professor means that under each major heading you should include two to four brief paragraphs describing clearly the content of that section. Professor warns you to pay particular attention to the logical flow of ideas from one section to the next. Professor wants a draft of this skeleton plan a week from today, at which time the two of you will review and modify it, and then you'll later elaborate on it before showing it to the client.

Independent 15 : 1

Review what you did in Assignments 1:1, 2 and 3, 4:1, 8:1, 9:1, 10:1, 11:1, 13:1 and 14:1. Your major department needs a basic communication plan. Review everything known about the department. Maybe you should again interview the department head. Write a skeleton communication plan, meaning that under each major heading you should include two to four brief paragraphs describing clearly the content of that section. Begin the plan with the department's mission and move forward. Pay particular attention to the logical flow of ideas from one section to the next. This skeleton plan should be complete by a week from today, at which time you should review it with the head of the department.

All Scenarios 15 : 2

You're busy at work when I. M. Professor pops into your office area and asks if the client has a fully developed media kit? When you nod your head negatively, Professor says that he's just talked with the management people who want a complete media kit plan as soon as possible. There's no deadline as such, but the client is anxious to have something in the can in case a crisis arises or some other event demands a news conference for some reason. Right now, all they have are a few isolated pieces of information but there's no plan for a kit to which staff people can refer for guidance. Using your knowledge of the client, Professor asks that you develop a media kit plan for general guidance of the client. That means that some special efforts will need to be made to prepare backgrounders, position papers, and so on for ready use. What Professor wants is an item-for-item list of things that should go into the kit. Provide one or two descriptive sentences for each item. Also, think of special occasions, such as a crisis, and provide guidelines for media kits in these situations. Professor wants this material by the end of the week, typed or word-processed double spaced.

Independent 15 : 2

Your university does not have a media kit. Interview the director of public relations and pick up as many pieces of information as you can. Consider the nature of the University and its constituents. Develop a general outline for a media kit, including a descriptive sentence or two for each item that should be included. Consider what might be needed if a crisis or other special event calls for a news conference or related activities.

Notes

Quick-Study

16

Extract, Chapter 15, "Speeches and Other Presentations,"
Public Relations Writing: Form & Style 6e, Belmont, California: Wadsworth, 2001.

Speeches and presentations have two things in common for the public relations writer. First is the impression the audience gets and second is what information it will retain. It is also wise to remember that speeches and presentations are also strategic tools. In that sense, you must ask yourself what strategic function does a speech or presentation serve in the context of fulfilling an organizational goal? From the point of view of business strategy, what does your organization expect as a result? Functional strategy is how the speech or presentation fits into the overall communication tactics of your organization. What effects are expected from the various publics who will be exposed directly to the speech or presentation?

Delivering a speech can be a hazardous task because it takes place in real time—just once. There's no room for correcting mistakes. For this reason, writing a speech, perhaps, demands more attention and care than any other form of public relations writing. One of the cardinal rules is that the speaker must sound natural. If you're writing for yourself, naturalness should come easy but when you're writing for others you'll have to work very hard to find just the right words and phrases unique to that person. For that to happen, you need to know a good bit of what the audience knows about the topic, the language members use when talking about it and what they expect from listening to the speech.

Public relations writers usually deal with just four basic types of speeches—informative, persuasive, entertaining and technical. A fifth type is called brief remarks, usually given on special occasions as expressions of thanks, welcome or acceptance. Whatever the type, the first step in good speech writing is planning. You'll likely develop a list of several good topics but these will be pared to just one after you've done your research. Then it is a matter of reducing the topic to just three main points that you want the audience to understand and retain. Of course, persuasion is an implicit part of every speech. Do you want the audience to take specific action, change its opinions about something or do you simply want to reinforce what the audience already knows and believes?

A speech has three main parts: introduction, body and conclusion. Start with a title. Keep in mind what you want the audience to do, say or adopt. Select only three main points you want to make in the speech. List these points on separate sheets of paper. Study them carefully and devise a theme that ties them together in some provocative way under the title. Develop a list of key words, concepts, anecdotes and so on for each of the three main points. Now you can write the body and conclusion. Then turn your attention to writing an introduction that leads the audience into the body. You need to concentrate on vivid words and expressive language. Be clear. Choose your words with precision. Be specific. Repeat each of the three main points at least three times, although never in the same way. That's where anecdotes and analogies are very useful. Involve the audience by using personal pronouns and posing questions that audience members can answer to themselves. If visuals are to be part of the speech, make sure the copy the speaker has is carefully coded to show cues for the visuals and a one- or two-word label of content. Having finished the speech, your task now is to write an introduction of the speaker. How the speaker is introduced can have an important impact on the effectiveness of the speech. Keep it short, simple and easy to read. When these things are done, your last task is to prepare a news release about the speech.

Unlike a speech that is given to a single audience in real time, other presentations are not tailored as specifically for a single audience or event. In that sense, other presentations may be seen *individually* (for example, when an employee plays a video about job benefits) or *collectively* (for example, when global sales forces see in their own groups in real time a video report from the CEO). Presentations also have a longer shelf life than speeches. You should approach script planning by first defining what you want to accomplish. Then consider the various publics who may see the presentation. For each of these publics, make a list of what each knows and needs to know about the topic. If potential publics are diverse, the task of doing an effective presentation is more complex, but not impossible with good planning and execution.

Most presentations other than speeches are *informational*. Many are directed to employees, organizational advisory groups, governmental regulatory or supervisory bodies or non-governmental groups (NGOs) who are special publics because of their interest in issues related to an organization, educational institution or association, trade or professional group. *Persuasive* presentations also may be directed to these groups, but these are mostly calls to action or they advance a point of view.

Planning focuses first on the main ideas you want to convey. List the key ideas on separate sheets of paper as you would when planning a speech. Fill in below each one points of information that must be conveyed. Arrange the key ideas so they flow logically, each one providing a natural progression to the next point. Use narrative to say what you want to say down the right half of each page. Once the narrative portion is done, go back and work down the left side and detail visuals, scenes and sound effects needed to reinforce each point at the right. In that sense, writing a presentation script is more like writing a play or a television commercial than writing a speech. Beyond those points, you want to include drama that builds to an ending that urges people to act, accept or retain the information.

Computerized presentation software makes it easier to see how words and images fit together. Even when you use this software, you'll also probably need to work closely with a graphic artist to come up with unique visuals that tell the story better than canned art. The right visuals can set a memorable mood, inject drama and explain words in powerful ways. Words in the script should help visuals do this. Be careful not to overwrite—a major problem with many presentation scripts. Presentation software offers a lot of flexibility. Words and images can be stored easily for later review and modification. Editing is simplified and printed copies of various versions can be produced easily and quickly. Computer-mediated presentations use a computer, a color LCD panel and a high density overhead projector or the computer can be connected directly to a large screen monitor. If the presentation will be made in a location that is not computer-capable, copies can be made from the computer and delivered on overhead cells or on 35mm slides. In spite of the usefulness of computer technology, there can be problems with it. Equipment can malfunction. Always have redundant equipment available and someone who has the technical skills to fix the problem quickly. Another problem is that software offers a dazzling array of techniques to present information. Be wary. Choose one and use it consistently. Too many variations confuse an audience.

Exercises Exercises **Exercises** Exercises

GEI 16 : 1

The Serene Chamber of Commerce wants to produce an economic development plan for the city and surrounding areas, capitalizing on some of the area's primary assets. Heddon T. Clouds, chair of the economic development committee, has invited Dr. Glen Kowan, CEO at GenEcon, to make a speech to the committee and all members of the Chamber and City Council at a special dinner meeting the third Monday of next month at

6:30 P.M. Clouds has suggested to Kowan that he talk about GenEcon's philosophy, the research staff and to speculate on the future of biotechnology as an economic force. Clouds also wants Kowan to offer an evaluation of the possibilities of attracting other biotechnology firms to the area. Kowan has agreed to Clouds' request. Kowan has asked I. M. Professor to develop a suitable speech. Professor, in turn, then assigns that task to you. Review what is known about GenEcon and biotechnology. Kowan is an accomplished speaker, so he can probably handle any speech quite well. He did tell Professor that he wanted visuals to supplement the speech and these could be a PowerPoint presentation or he's adept at using overhead cells. Professor wants a draft of the speech no later than two weeks from today. The draft should include a title, about two pages of copy from the body of the speech, and the rest can be in outline form. Please include a schedule of visuals you think might be appropriate. The speech should be 20-25 minutes, leaving some time for questions and answers.

NATS 16 : 1

Overcrowding in hospital emergency rooms has grown progressively worse. The management of NATS and its members are deeply concerned. That's why Dr. H. Arthur (Arty) Hart, executive director of NATS, recently approached the leadership of the American Medical Association and asked for a plenary session on the problem at the next AMA convention. The AMA reception was a little tepid but it agreed to a 40-minute PowerPoint presentation, leaving 25 minutes or so for questions and answers. Dr. Hart has asked I. M. Professor to assign a ProCom staff member to produce a draft of a speech. Professor assigns the speech to you. You need to concentrate on learning as much as possible about the problem. Work the Internet and go to the library. The AMA expects Dr. Hart to propose some form of action the AMA could take. Professor wants a rough draft two weeks from now. It should have a title and about two pages of the body of the speech. The rest can be in outline form. Also, include suggested visuals that might accompany the speech. The AMA convention draws more than 4,000 physicians to its annual meetings, so the audience will be large. That may influence the number and kinds of visuals you suggest.

NCCC 16 : 1

Child care has become more and more of a problem for working parents, especially those in the upper-lower and lower-middle economic classes. The child development model used by the Diaperchanges to launch

NCCC prices this kind of child care out of reach for many parents. And the cost to parents to get their children into NCCC programs is increasingly hard on some parents. The leadership of BABY, now the principal owner of NCCC, wants to promote developmental day care centers on a broader scale. Manford Z. Topper, chief executive officer of BABY, contacted the president of the National Association of Child Psychologists, requesting to speak to the NACP about the problem at the association's next convention. The NACP executive board approved the request. Topper believes that members of NACP can be influential in their own communities in getting other child care centers to adopt a developmental model for the children in their care. However, this will drive up their costs, so they may not be responsive. However, Topper has been working closely with congressional leaders in Washington to make government money available so costs for developmental child care can be more affordable. The political reason for this program is that it is less expensive to give good care to youngsters than it is to house them in jails or reform schools later on in life. Topper has asked I. M. Professor for help in getting the speech ready for the NACP. Professor assigns this task to you. Research child care programs and their costs. Seek authorities who can testify that a modest investment in developmental child care pays big dividends by avoiding other costs. About 500 psychologists will be at the meeting. Professor wants a rough draft of a 25-minute speech in two weeks. It should include a title, about two pages of the body, and the rest can be in outline form. Topper prefers visuals and a projected outline of his talk on an LCD panel.

Independent 16 : 1

Your major department needs a 10-minute video to be used as a recruiting tool. Since you're enrolled for credit in a projects course with the chair, you get to do a script for this video. Review all of the materials form the department and the University. These should give you some clues as to how you might approach this task. Recall the kinds of questions you had about the department as you considered becoming a major in it. Talk to other students, also, about the kinds of questions they had. You need not write a full script. An outline is acceptable, although one page of the script should be written.

Notes

Quick-Study

17

Extract, Chapter 17, "Newsletters,"
Public Relations Writing: Form & Style 6e, Belmont, California: Wadsworth, 2001.

Newsletters are hard to describe because they come in all sizes and shapes and their range of purposes defies easy classification. But they all must meet certain criteria if they are successful. Specifically they must:

1. Fill an unmet need.

2. Convey information in some unique way so that people will pay attention to them.

3. Be distributed in a way that is efficient and regularly reaches intended audiences.

4. Do things for their audiences other media can't.

5. Have a person or staff interested in and skilled enough to properly produce them.

6. Be issued frequently enough that their content remains timely in the eyes of their readers.

By definition, newsletters are serial publications. They must have volume numbers and issue numbers and be issued at stated intervals.

The primary purpose of any newsletter is to communicate regularly with members of a group. Sharing relevant information is a principal way an organization sustains itself. This is as true of a firm and its relations with employees as it is for members of a group bound together only by a special interest.

Newsletters are important media for *internal communication*. Good managers use newsletters as an important means to increase understanding and support of employees. Good employee newsletters have sharply focused content that is selected and written to emphasize what is going on inside the organization. Information from the outside is also included if it affects what goes on inside, especially the way employees do their jobs. Employee newsletters also try to humanize the workplace. They do this by calling attention to employee accomplishments that may include recognition for things not related to their jobs. Humor is sometimes used, also, to help humanize the organization, but this has to be done with skill for three reasons. First, humor goes stale quickly. Second, humor can be a beguiling trap that leads to gossip. And third, humor can blind writers to the sensitive personal feelings of the people they write about.

Special interest subscriber newsletters serve audiences who are bound by common interests other than employee-employer. One category of special interest newsletters is *lifestyles*. These newsletters convey information to a group of people who enjoy doing the same kind of things, such as flying, scuba diving, gardening, attending symphonic concerts and so on. Rarely do newsletters of this type have content that is not directly related to the area of special interest. *Economic* newsletters are, as the name implies, focused on economic issues. The spectrum of these letters is enormous. They may be produced and distributed free by a bank, for example, or they may be profit-making enterprises, such as *The Mutual Fund Letter.* Some newsletters are available on the Web. Some subscriber newsletters are delivered regularly to all members with e-mail addresses.

Political parties and most politicians at all levels use newsletters as a way of staying in touch with their constituents. In some cases, *political* newsletters are used also for fund-raising. Their very essence is to assert and reinforce the "party line." Newsletters dealing with *religion* are found in local churches as well as at the denominational level. Those circulating at the regional or national level often focus on broad social or doctrinal issues and are written with a doctrinaire tone. *Social* newsletters include a broad range of communication efforts. If you're in a sorority or fraternity, you'll likely get its newsletter long after you leave campus, provided you pay your dues. On the other hand, social newsletters can also include such newsletters as from the local Rotary or the Business and Professional Women. *Professional* newsletters are represented by such publications as *pr reporter*, *PR News* and *O'Dwyer's Newsletter*. Engineers, certified public accountants and urologists, among thousands of professions, all have newsletters that try to keep them abreast of the latest information regarding their fields.

Technical issues involve three major points. First, distinguish between reporting and writing. Reporting deals with the gathering of information. Writing deals with analyzing and packaging it. Getting useful, unique information is essential if you expect to develop and hold a select audience, as illustrated by a newsletter like the *Back Pain Monitor.* Second, there is less room for mistakes in newsletters than in any other medium because your audience is sophisticated regarding the topic of the newsletter. Mistakes are spotted quickly by audiences, and these readers are not very forgiving. Third, you must adopt and observe a hard-news policy. People don't subscribe to a newsletter like the *Mutual Fund Letter* for entertainment.

Writing in most newsletters is bare-bones. It mostly uses the traditional subject-verb-object pattern. Adjectives and adverbs are scarce. Compound sentences are uncommon. In sum, the writing is Spartan. Although the five Ws and H of newswriting can be found in newsletters, one of these elements dominates the content. For example, if your newsletter focuses on entertainment celebrities, the "who" will be important throughout your newsletter.

You must understand clearly how your audience uses, or expects to use, your newsletter. Otherwise, you will have difficulty defining an appropriate purpose. Distribution can have an impact on how you design your newsletter. If you intend it to be a self-mailer, it must carry your return address, postage and the name of the addressee. Always check with the postmaster at the site where the newsletter will be mailed to clarify rules and regulations of the U.S. Postal Service. If your newsletter is likely to be filed or inserted into ring binders, most audiences prefer one that is standard letter size. A letter-size format also works well if the newsletter will be posted for others to read. Larger formats may be needed, especially if you use much art.

If you're writing and designing on a desktop computer system, you have quick access to many helpful aids. One is that you have a *word processor* that speeds up the editorial process. It makes it possible to check and recheck facts up to the last minute before reproduction. Word processors also have *spell checkers* that help you to avoid spelling errors. However, they will OK poor word choice if the word is spelled correctly. *Thesauruses* help you locate just the right synonym or antonym. But you must still exercise good judgment that the word suggested is the most appropriate one for the context in which it is used. Remember that the computer is blind to *homophones.* If you spell the word as *rain* or *reign* but mean *rein,* you have used the wrong word, although it is spelled correctly. *Grammar* software is also available, but it is not much help to a reasonably skilled writer. However, some of this software can help you to identify passive voice easily. That is very helpful.

Designing a newsletter is also helped by a desktop system. One issue that has to be settled early is the format. Because the leading design software lets you easily experiment with and change formats, don't get caught in the trap of putting out editions that look as if they're not related. Settle on a design scheme, make templates of it and use it consistently. Resist the temptation to use art for art's sake. If it is not directly related to content, don't use it, and then only if it helps understanding. Study and practice with your design software every day. Exercise restraint regarding type selection. Use a traditional serif type for text, and avoid sans serif type. Use a compatible serif or sans serif type for display. Some sans serif display faces work really well with traditional text fonts. Although stories should have been written to fit, you can modify spacing so that stories fit more precisely into your design. Never let space interfere with content.

Exercises Exercises **Exercises** Exercises

GEI 17 : 1

One of the first things Drewhurst did when she came to GEI was to design a newsletter, called *GEI News*, to be distributed monthly. She's budgeted to cover 12 issues annually, using a second color in each issue with up to 12 pages in a letter-size format. It is folded once so that the bottom half of the back page contains room for the return address, mailing permit and space for mailing labels. Although the newsletter's primary audiences are employees, members of the advisory board and life scientists at State University, it is also circulated to the business, political and cultural leaders in Serene. It is also mailed to all vendors and to similar research laboratories around the world. Neither Drewhurst nor other management team members are satisfied with its content or look.

Candidly, Drewhurst has no better than average writing skills and she does not have a good feel for what makes good newsletter copy. She also isn't very skilled with design, although she's technically adept with both PageMaker and Quark Express. She just does not have the "eye" to do consistently good design. She talked with Professor more than two hours yesterday, asking advice about what to do with the newsletter.

Professor suggested that she let ProCom develop a design prototype that Drewhurst could use as a template. The intent is that ProCom would do about four versions of the same basic design so that Drewhurst would have some variety in design yet retain the same general appearance. Professor also agreed that ProCom will develop a list of story types that Drewhurst can look for every month. This list will contain many more story ideas than can be used in a single issue, perhaps as many as four issues. The list is really a shopping list that Drewhurst can use to guide her newsgathering efforts.

Professor assigns you this task for GEI. You are expected to submit a basic design. If it is satisfactory, then variations can be developed later. Professor also wants you to develop a list of story topics that Drewhurst can use. Be prepared to talk with Drewhurst at length about what these ideas can lead to. Professor wants these two projects by Friday noon.

NCCC 17 : 1

After buying NCCC, BABY rapidly expanded the number of centers and divided up territories into regions. As the organization grew, BABY leadership found it increasingly difficult to keep NCCC people abreast of what was going on in the organization. Their primary means had been letters and memos to local management, but rarely to other employees. They relied primarily on posters on bulletin boards for policy announcements. BABY now wants to begin the production of an internal newsletter. After negotiations with Terry Childers, ProCom has drawn the assignment to come up with editorial and design schemes for it. Professor assigns you this task and says that "a complete draft should be ready for us to discuss by this time next week." Name the newsletter, list information categories that should go into it and come up with a workable design.

NATS 17 : 1

NATS has a monthly newsletter, *Traumatic*, that focuses on research findings in brief, the association's lobbying efforts at the state and national levels and interpretations of and opinions about proposed legislation that may affect emergency care. The NATS leadership now wants to produce a second monthly newsletter. This new one will focus on the people who provide emergency care. The idea behind this new newsletter is to humanize the process for NATS members. The thinking is that the stress level is so high among people who work in emergency medicine that a newsletter is needed whose content is very personal, empathetic and inspiring, thus making people feel better about themselves and their work. That may be a far-fetched goal, but NATS wants to try it. So ProCom has been asked to come up with a name, an editorial treatment and a design for this newsletter. Professor assigns it to you and says, "I want a complete draft by this time next week so that we can discuss it in great detail."

Independent 17 : 1

Get a copy of each of the last three issues of the alumni newsletter at your university. Review its basic design. Write a critique of the design, and propose an alternate design that you believe will be better. Do a draft design to support your proposal.

Notes

Quick-Study

18

Extract, Chapter 18, "Brochures," *Public Relations Writing: Form & Style* 6e
Belmont, California: Wadsworth, 2001.

The term *brochure* is used two ways. When used in the broad sense, it includes *booklets, flyers, circulars, leaflets, pamphlets or tracts*, as well as brochures. Used in the narrow sense, it means a printed piece of six or more pages, published once and distributed to special publics for a single purpose. By whatever name, brochures have some things in common:

1. Message statements are always singular.
2. Their purpose is to persuade, inform and/or educate.
3. They are published only once, but multiple printings of some are common.
4. They must attract and hold their own audiences.
5. They are their own delivery systems (they aren't parts of other media).
6. Clear writing and attractiveness are essential.

The first step in writing and designing is to define the *purpose*. What do you really want to do? If you can't answer that with a simple, declarative sentence, think about it some more. Is it to *persuade*? If so, the writing is much like advertising copy. The difference is that brochure and Web page copy is usually longer, and it leans heavily on adjectives, similes and metaphors. Is it to *educate* or *inform*? If so, it must appeal to the cognitive behavior of readers. That means that you will write copy that is more fact-intensive and descriptive.

Developing a creative *concept* is the next step. A good concept takes a key idea and interprets it, shapes it and, in turn, is shaped by it, and produces a fully coordinated message that blends the elements into a cohesive unit so that the whole is a sum greater than its parts. To develop a creative concept, begin with the brochure's purpose and add an object or an application to it. You'll want the concept to be *unique*, so that it is memorable. If you stretch too hard, however, to make the concept unique you may resort to *cleverness* that becomes trite. Resist the temptation to use *puff* words like *best*, *richest*, *prettiest* and *lowest*, because you want to be believable.

Writing is actually the third step in the process. Always observe the *rules of* good *grammar*, *punctuation* and *spelling*. Be absolutely *accurate* in what you say and show. Generally use active voice, although passive voice is permissible if it helps you say something with more clarity. Conform to a specific *style*, and use it consistently. Good brochure copy sets a proper *tone* for what is being said. You also must paint pictures with words. Having written the copy, go back and think about the visuals you'll want to accompany the copy. Generally, if you can use a visual instead of a paragraph, do it. There are two types of visuals. One is *line* art. It is black and white, with no shades of gray. The other is *screened* or *halftone* art. Art that must show gradations of tone—a photograph, for example—must be screened; that is, the image is broken up into a series of dots so that it will reproduce properly.

Creating a *design* includes several major issues. *Format* deals with the size and shape of pages although in Web pages the format is confined to the shape of the screen, as well as their number. The use of *type* probably is the area where inexperience shows most. Generally, select a traditional *serif* font for text and a *san serif* font for display. *Paper* is another area where inexperience may be obvious in brochures you produce. Generally, the best advice is to consult an expert on paper stock. But there are several concepts you need to know. One is that paper has *grain*. The fibers run in one direction and fold better in that direction. The *basis weight* of paper refers to the weight of 500 sheets of paper cut from basic stock. For example, standard business letterheads are usually on 20-lb stock, meaning 500 sheets of 17-by-22 inches, quartered to 8.5-by-11 inches. *Curl* refers to the extent paper will buckle because of excessive moisture. *Paper-ink affinity* refers to how quickly ink dries on printed stock. The *color* of paper can affect readability. A block of text is usually easiest to read on a soft (yellowish) white stock. If you're using four-color process, however, go to a neutral white stock. *Brightness* of paper affects the brilliance, contrast and sparkle of printed images. A *smooth* paper is needed if you're printing letterpress or gravure. Paper also comes in *grades*. Those you're most concerned with are *bond* (typical correspondence paper), *coated* (highest quality reproduction), *text* (flyers, brochures and announcements), *book* (trade and textbooks), *offset* (less moisture absorbent because of the printing method) and *cover* (heavier stock used for covers).

White space is as much an element of design as type or art. Fundamental decisions involve the kinds of margins you'll use, the line lengths of type and how much space there will be between columns of text, how much white space will appear around art and whether you'll use bleeds (running printed material off the edge of the paper). Never run type into the margins. As elements are arranged within the framework of a page, be careful not to trap white space inside. Always leave an opening to the outside.

Color can help the appearance of brochures as well as Web pages, but it often does not help retention of or responses to messages. There are two kinds of color for use in brochures. One is *spot* color. This involves the use of another (or second) color, in addition to the basic color of ink used (usually black). If yet another color is used, it is called a third color. Spot color is not *close-register* and is therefore less expensive to prepare and print. With careful, knowledgeable use of screens and tint blocks, you can get a rainbow of effects for a modest investment. *Four-color* process, however, is much more expensive. That's because the art must be shot and screened four times to filter out all but the primary colors—yellow, red, blue and black. Separate printing plates are made of each of these, and four passes are made on the printing press to apply those colors in sequence, one on top of the last one. It is close-register printing because each dot of the image must align perfectly over the one below it. Otherwise, the image is out of focus.

How you *reproduce* the brochure may influence your design and other elements, such as paper stock. You have three options. First, you may use *letterpress*, noted for its crisp images. It prints from a raised surface. Second, you may use *offset*, a method that prints from a flat surface. It works on the principle that oil and water don't mix. It is noted for soft, smooth transitions of color and tones. *Gravure* prints from a recessed surface, and it is known for the highest quality of reproduction. It also is usually the most expensive.

Distribution is the last major part of creating an effective brochure. Although it is discussed last, that does not mean that it is unimportant. In fact, define clearly how the brochure will be distributed before you begin writing and designing. If it will be mailed in a standard business envelop, that influences the number and size of pages. If the brochure is to be a self-mailer, you must design a mailing panel that has the return address and a place for postage (or a mail permit), as well as space for an addressee. If it is to be displayed in racks, the slots in the racks limit the size of the pages, and it must be printed on stock that is stiff enough not to buckle.

Exercises Exercises **Exercises** Exercises

GEI 18 : 1

As you know, GEI is a start-up. It isn't well known in the community of Serene or in the research community nationally or globally, although many of its scientists have outstanding reputations. Drewhurst is fully aware of this problem. That's one reason she earlier had asked ProCom to do a plan for a Web site (review what you did in Assignment 14:1) which is now being built. She now thinks that one of the things GEI should do is to develop a high quality brochure. Staff scientists at GEI are enthusiastic. In fact, one of the scientists has suggested that the brochure design include a special pocket so results of the most recent research completed at GenEcon can be inserted. In that sense, the brochure will parallel GenEcon's Web site, although new inserts will not be produced as often as updates are made to the Web site. Drewhurst intends to circulate the brochure among leadership groups in Serene and surrounding towns. It will also be distributed selectively to scientists active in biotechnology research. Kowan has also noted that the brochure can be an effective tool when he's recruiting new staff.

Drewhurst believes that the development of an effective brochure should get high priority. She met with Professor earlier today and asked for ProCom's expertise in creating the brochure, including typical content and the design itself. Because of the demand on Drewhurst's time, it is probable that ProCom will be asked to do the inserts used to update the brochure.

Professor asked you to take on this assignment. What you are expected to do is to work up a creative plan for the design and content of the brochure for GEI. Do two versions of a rough draft design and include two or three sample blocks of copy that give the flavor of the finished brochure. Professor wants this by Friday noon before a scheduled talk with Drewhurst about the brochure later that day. If there is general agreement on your basic plan, developmental work will follow.

NCCC 18 : 1

NCCC's experimental arrangement with State University seems to be working well. The center has been open for three months and was filled to capacity by the middle of the second month of operations.

Surveys show client families have high regard for the way their children are being treated. Focus group interviews with parents have uncovered stories of positive changes in the behavior of their children. A benchmark survey of students, staff and faculty about their child-care needs two months before the center opened showed a general lack of high regard for the services then available in Serene. Results of another survey released yesterday shows client families to be highly favorable toward the NCCC campus program.

Discussions with State University leaders have also been positive. And because there is already a long waiting list of potential clients, NCCC is considering expanding the State University facility, although no final decision has been made. All the signs, however, have prompted NCCC management to look even harder at its long-range objective of developing centers on other campuses.

A basic step in marketing these centers on other campuses is to prepare a brochure that showcases the State University center and its success. NCCC wants ProCom to develop a basic concept for this brochure, along with a tentative design and some sample copy. It really isn't looking for a finished brochure because a decision to go national on this project is still a year or so away. NCCC simply wants to get its plan worked out in detail so that it can be implemented quickly and effectively if a positive decision is made. ProCom assigns you this task because you've worked so success-fully on other NCCC projects. NCCC has imposed no restrictions.

The only instruction from Sully Trotter is "We want to do it right. We want to showcase this idea and make it so compelling that campus admin-istrators will beat a path to our door, once they've seen our brochure." Because this is a speculative task for NCCC, check with your ProCom supervisor about the deadline.

NATS 18 : 1

The NATS leadership is committed to the idea that the best solution to the emergency medical care problem is to prevent the need for it. That's why NATS values highly the position paper you did as Assignment 8:1. But NATS is also realistic enough to know that even generally preventable accidents may sometimes happen.

So NATS has asked ProCom to produce a brochure that details step-by-step procedures to be used until professional emergency medical special-ists are on the scene. NATS wants this brochure to focus on nine trauma situations: (1) cardiac arrest, (2) automobile accidents, (3) poisoning, (4) burns, (5) smoke inhalation, (6) heat stroke, (7) drowning, (8) choking and (9) gunshot and stab wounds.

Because of the cost of printing and distributing millions of copies of this brochure, NATS wants it done in a single color on inexpensive stock. Although appearance is important, NATS is more concerned about content and the creative use of simple visuals to illustrate first-aid procedures.

Because this project will tax its resources, NATS has asked ProCom to develop a concept for the brochure, a tentative design and some sample copy. If there is a favorable review, the brochure will be fully developed and bids taken for its production. NATS is eager to get an early look at what ProCom recommends. Check with your supervisor for a deadline.

Independent 18 : 1

Brochures are fairly common in the departments of many universities. They explain the nature of departmental programs and the personnel (faculty and staff) and facilities and equipment available to support these programs. The intent of most of these brochures, even if unstated, is to recruit students to these programs.

The situation at your University is an uneven mix of materials. Some departments have brochures. Some are elaborate. Others are quite modest. Your department has no brochure at the moment, but the head of the program wants one. Law prohibits use of state funds for brochures. So private funds must be used, and these are limited.

There is enough money to produce an 8.5-by-11 inch bifold brochure on plain stock, perhaps with a second color. The estimated press run is 5,000 copies. Because money is tight, the department head has asked around for names of people who could undertake this project. She or he has settled on you.

You should get a university catalog, a few brochures from other departments and some copies of memos and letters that talk about the objectives and philosophy that drive the department's programs. Using this information as a base, interview the department head and a sampling of faculty and students, probing for points of view, strengths and weaknesses and so on until you have a good feel for what should be put into the brochure. Develop a brochure concept. Then write and design it.

Notes

Quick-Study

Extract, Chapter 19, " Magazines and Annual Reports,"
Public Relations Writing: Form & Style 6e, Belmont, California: Wadsworth, 2001.

Doing a feature for an employee magazine is probably one of the most enjoyable writing jobs in public relations. But not all writers handle feature materials well. They sometimes get so involved in the corporate culture that their stories fall flat because they have lost touch with their audiences. So the first rule about this type of writing is not only to know your audience, but to stay tuned in to what interests it most, and why. Before reading further, review Chapter 11, "Features for Print and Broadcasting," in *PRW6e.*

Finding story ideas is usually not difficult, but evaluating them may be. The key question is, Is the audience interested in this idea? A practical problem sometimes arises when you know a story is interesting to the audience but management does not want you to treat the topic. What are the politics of getting an idea cleared? What are the consequences of this story? Even if a story does not have high interest, its consequences may make it an important one to write. Employees should know the company line or position even if they are not interested in it.

If you write the story, give special attention to developing a good angle. An angle is simply a point of view that comes through clearly. It must go beyond simply writing about a topic like federal safety standards—one that can cure insomnia. You need an angle. A good angle for federal safety standards might deal with ways to handle and dispose of toxic wastes, which also scores high in consequences, especially if your company deals with toxic waste disposal.

If you've chosen a good angle, the next problem is to overcome writing errors caused by sloppy or incomplete research. To refresh yourself on PR writing research, review Chapter 4 of *PRW6e.* Focus first on your topic's background. Develop a broad data base, then narrow it and pursue in-depth information. Interview experts in the field.

The article's lead must get the interest of readers and tell them what the story is about. It should state the article's central point. Readers won't devote much time searching for the central point. So don't bury it. Put it up front, and rely on the body of the story to hold onto the readers the lead has captured.

The body supports and explains the central point. It amplifies, interprets, verifies and illustrates. Use anecdotes to sustain interest by giving readers something to visualize. Anecdotes show readers instead of merely telling them. Anecdotes also humanize stories. And direct quotes make stories more personal and livelier.

Description is especially important when you're writing about something unfamiliar to your audience. Writing good description can be difficult. As a rule of thumb, describe the unfamiliar with the familiar. Employee magazines often copy the news release style of writing.

Members of associations often feel a strong sense of identity. They look to the association's magazine or other publication to give them a continuous stream of relevant information relative to their interest in the association.

Trade and industry magazines have little general interest to people outside those fields. But to people in those trades or industries, these magazines represent a major source of current information about what is going on. Such magazines are often on the forefront of documenting technological changes, trends and developments that may be of major importance to these groups. Because the audiences of these magazines have so much expertise in their fields, even the smallest mistake can be very damaging.

Still another kind of specialized magazine is the corporate magazine designed to be read by its publics. These magazines often are used to promote product lines. For example, Sony uses *Sony Style* to promote its electronic gear. *Sony Style* is intended to cement brand loyalty by giving customers a steady diet of useful information that helps them get the most from their electronic devices. Another purpose is to use corporate magazines to create, sustain and polish image.

Annual reports often look like magazines, but that appearance is deceiving. Publicly owned firms must issue annual reports, and federal requirements say these reports must be clear and accurate. Many other firms issue these reports because they think they should. But sometimes firms don't really want to explain clearly how they are doing, so they obscure the facts. Their reports may be technically accurate, but the writing is so burdened with conditional clauses and big words that hardly anyone knows or cares what they say.

One problem with the writing in annual reports is that the copy must be cleared through many levels and people. In the process, a simple, direct sentence or a whole article may get changed into a piece of fuzzy, indirect writing.

Annual reports are rarely assigned to inexperienced writers. You may help with an annual report in your first job, but your role will be limited to gathering basic information and the like. Although they are larger projects, preparing annual reports can be approached much as you would prepare a brochure.

Annual reports attempt two things: (1) to provide investors with basic data about firms and (2) to describe operations and prospects for the future. Annual reports are written for select audiences, but rarely for just one or two. Develop a complete list of audiences. Don't be surprised if you have a list of 20 or more. Study the list carefully to determine which groups are essential to the success of your firm. Write your report to those few groups.

There is no absolute inventory of content for an annual report, but a key element is the *executive's letter*. Another is the *narrative*, in which you tell the organization's story in detail. It should give a general description of the company or institution; its location, purposes, products and services; and its related activities. It should amplify what happened last year and project the future, even if the executive's letter mentions them. The narrative must also disclose and describe events, management decisions, sales, mergers or conditions that have had, or will have, important effects on operations.

The most successful annual reports often make strong thematic statements. A good theme can be the creative glue that binds diverse pieces of information. It also can give the impression that a firm is highly organized and managed well.

Annual reports may range from modest to elaborate, but their preparation and production stretch over several months. Commonly, six or seven months will elapse from the time of the first planning meeting until the annual report is distributed. Many companies now use considerably abbreviated annual reports since these, and the 10K, are available electronically.

Special Note

It is acceptable in assignment 19:1 to create attribution and quotes as you need them, a fairly common practice in the field. However, common practice is also to clear all attributions and quotes by the persons named before stories are released.

Two different audiences are involved in the following assignments. Review the referenced materials carefully to pick up points of view that are especially relevant to each audience, and feature those angles. Refer to what you did in Assignments 8:1, 9:1, 10:1, 11:1, 13:1, 17:1 and 18:1 before you begin work.

GEI 19 : 1

Do two feature stories on the redesign of GEI's newsletter. Do one story first for the *Clarion* and another for a magazine of your choice. Evaluate the audiences that will read these stories. Orient your stories to those audiences.

NATS 19 : 1

Do two feature stories, one for a state trade magazine and one for a national magazine like the one published by the American Automobile Association. The focus should be on the new NATS newsletter that focuses on people who provide emergency care. Your point of view should come through clearly:

NCCC 19 : 1

Do two feature stories, one for a national magazine like *Parents* and one that is business oriented, such as the magazine produced by the U.S. Chamber of Commerce. Review materials carefully to glean information and points of view that are especially relevant to these diverse readers.

Independent 19 : 1

Do two feature stories, one for the student newspaper and one for the university's alumni magazine. Examine carefully the information you developed for Assignment 9:1 from the points of view of these diverse audiences, and write specifically to them. Although each group of readers may be interested in the university, their interests are motivated by different concerns. Make sure you know these differences before you begin writing.

GEI 19 : 2

GEI has not issued an annual report because it is such a young organization. However, Drewhurst has convinced Kowan that it is good policy for GEI to begin planning for an annual report to come out about 1.5 years after the founding of the organization. GEI is not required to issue an annual report because it is a privately held company. But the nature of the work at GEI suggests that an annual report is in the public interest. If it is done well, Drewhurst and the management team believe it can be a showcase for GEI, its people and its projects. The advisory board endorsed the idea, also, but several members expressed doubts. They seemed to have had trouble justifying the costs of doing the kind of report Drewhurst has in mind.

Drewhurst wants a report on coated stock, 8.5-by-11 inches, 24 pages plus cover and with about 20 four-color process graphics—a mix of pictures, art and graphs. She recognizes that she cannot do good design and that her writing and editing skills are no better than average. That is why she contacted Professor. She wants to retain ProCom to write, edit and produce GEI's annual report. Professor has agreed.

When you got to work this morning, there was a memo from Professor with the following instructions:

1. Bone up on the nature of annual reports.
2. Develop a creative plan for GEI's first-ever annual report.
3. Do a prototype design of four pages that gives a clear view of what the report will look like.

4. Develop a skeleton outline of the content of the report.

Professor wants this by noon Monday in order to be ready for a planning conference with Drewhurst.

NATS 19 : 2

NATS produces a slim annual report for its membership. This document usually focuses on NATS's financial status, membership trends and recent public policy changes affecting emergency medicine. Because NATS has become proactive by educating people about the benefits of preventing accidents as a way of minimizing the need for emergency care, it decided yesterday to issue an annual report with a greater emphasis on public interest issues. Shortly after the NATS board made this decision, NATS called ProCom to explain the idea and to ask for ProCom's help.

A meeting is set between ProCom and NATS leadership next week for an initial discussion. Based on yesterday's phone call, your assignment is to conceptualize this annual report, produce a draft design and write some sample copy for it. As this assignment requires a quick turnaround, you'll need to review all the materials you've produced to date for NATS as well as any pertinent library materials.

Next week's meeting with the NATS people will probably result in several changes in what you propose, but that's expected. Go into this assignment with the idea that what you produce will not get approval without significant change. Final approval may not come until several meetings are held and you've gone through several design and writing treatments. Check with your ProCom supervisor for a deadline.

NCCC 19 : 2

Because the experimental child-care center at State University has proved so successful, NCCC is planning similar centers on six other campuses. Serious negotiations are under way at 22 other campuses. Formal announcement of agreements with most or all of these institutions are expected within the next two or three months. Several other campus administrations have shown tentative interest, but it is too early to tell which way they'll go.

NCCC seems to be riding the crest of considerable public recognition and respect. Several prominent educational journals have carried stories about the Serene center's effectiveness. So have some popular magazines, including *Time*. Associated Press has also done a lengthy series carried in many of the nation's daily newspapers.

NCCC wants to exploit this environment, so it has decided to produce an annual report that capitalizes on this interest in developmental child-care. It wants to persuade readers of the benefits to society for the type of centers NCCC is now operating at campus sites and to establish NCCC as *the* leader in child-care developmental centers. That shouldn't be difficult, given the kind of recent attention NCCC has gotten.

NCCC has turned, naturally, to ProCom to produce the report. And NCCC has specifically asked that you undertake the project. ProCom agrees and Professor suggests that you first develop a concept for the report, write some sample copy for it, and do a tentative design.

Your supervisor warns you not to get caught up in the euphoria surrounding NCCC's success at State University. Yes, there is a good story to tell, but stick with the facts. Facts seem to speak more persuasively than glittering generalities.

Independent 19 : 2

Conceptualize and write some sample copy, as well as create a basic design, for an annual report on student government programs on your campus. Plan this report for distribution to the *whole* university community, not just to students.

Review the structure of student governance, the nature of student programs and services and how the student government mechanisms relate to overall university governance. A key component, too, is how student government is funded and how it spends those funds. You may find it useful to do in-depth interviews with student government leaders and the principal administrators at your university.

Notes

Quick-Study

Extract, Chapter 20, "Crisis Communication,"
Public Relations Writing: Form & Style 6e, Belmont, California: Wadsworth, 2001.

Effective writing in a crisis situation is more a test of your preparation for a crisis than it is of your writing skills. Remember this important rule: Be prepared. As a writer, you may have no direct responsibility for issues management, but you must know which issues may induce a crisis. And you must know what the response plan is if a situation reaches crisis levels. Only if you are prepared can you put a writing strategy into motion quickly and effectively.

Begin your preparation by imagining a worst-case scenario, even if it pales in comparison with what happens. Ask yourself "what if" questions. Only when you can give quick, good responses to those questions are you ready to begin your preparation. You must resolve two important issues. First, plan carefully how to sustain the flow of accurate and current routine information *inside* the organization. Second, plan carefully how to sustain communication with groups *outside* your organization, including the media.

Responsible firms develop crisis plans. These plans detail who will do what under which circumstances. Plans must be reviewed regularly and be in the hands of people who have primary response roles. A key tenet of most crisis plans is to name two spokespersons. One is responsible for communicating inside and the other for communicating outside an organization. The two spokespersons must rehearse regularly how to behave when a crisis strikes. Although factual accuracy is always prized, its value is never so great as in a crisis because that's when it is most difficult to verify.

Crisis plans usually name a crisis management team, including those named as inside and outside spokespersons. The team usually includes a few key officers whose energies and skills will be devoted to managing the crisis. Other officers continue operations as normally as possible.

Your primary roles as a writer are to:

1. Create worst-case scenarios to which the crisis management team can respond.

2. Rehearse the two spokespersons on how to interact with the media during a crisis.

3. Explain carefully why the same information must be given to publics inside and outside the firm.

4. Rehearse other crisis team members who may interact with the media.

5. Have an adequate supply of documents nearby, such as facts sheets, position papers, backgrounders, biographies of key officers, pictures, maps, names, titles, addresses and phone numbers of key personnel (not just officers) and the like.

6. Anticipate where crisis command posts should be located and what facilities must be provided, such as phone lines, copy and fax machines, and the like.

7. Play the role of reporter covering a crisis. Ask difficult questions. By listening carefully to answers, you can be ready to respond to real questions when the occasion arises.

8. Call news conferences only on an as-needed basis.

The quality of your organization's leadership makes your job easier or more difficult during crisis situations. If leaders are open and candid, your job is easy, although contending with a crisis tends to mask this value until after a crisis is over. It is easier for you to take charge of the situation by sharing information quickly and freely. And your organization will come out better in the long run. Faced with questions that may represent security or legal issues, you're free to say, "I have the information, but I can't comment on that now."

Leaders who stonewall the media about a crisis make your role difficult. Reporters may try to trap you into revealing information. You and the organization may get pilloried because stonewalling is often interpreted as arrogant, not only by the media but also by affected publics. If reporters are stonewalled, everything you say after a crisis will be viewed with suspicion, which can stretch a crisis beyond its normal span.

GEI 20 : 1

Two lab assistants at GEI were accidentally exposed to a virus that attacks the central nervous system and can lead to permanent loss of motor skills, even to death in rare instances. The accident happened about two weeks ago, but the GEI management team and other lab personnel were determined to keep the accident and injuries from the public. When the two lab technicians were admitted to the Serene hospital for treatment, a guarded explanation was made to attending physicians so they would know what caused the problem.

As would be expected, the word began to spread among hospital workers and eventually it leaked to a reporter at the *Clarion*. The reporter immediately contacted Evelyn Drewhurst for verification. It is unfortunate that at the time of the accident GEI did not have a crisis management plan. When the accident became known among lab workers, the management team was concerned that they did not know how to handle the situation regarding the public. Drewhurst immediately contacted ProCom for assistance in drafting a crisis plan. Professor assigned you to develop the plan for GEI. Although the GEI management team has now approved the plan, expecting to modify it later because it was drawn under great stress, this approval gave Drewhurst some policy directions about how to proceed. She contacted Professor yesterday about the problem and asked ProCom to prepare a statement for release to the media and a news release for both print and broadcast distribution. That's when Professor assigned the task to you. You met with Ms. Drewhurst this morning and she cleared your statement and news releases after minor editing for use about two hours before the *Clarion* reporter called. By the way, the two lab technicians are responding well to treatment and a full recovery is expected. You'll want to quote Kowan as praising the medical expertise at Serene Hospital, both in the statement and in the news releases. Do three things:

1. Do a draft crisis plan for GEI.
2. Draft a statement from GEI regarding the accident for release to the media.
3. Draft a news release each for the *Clarion*, one radio and one television stations (your choice) .

NATS 20 : 1

A national magazine published a cover story about emergency medical care that says it is the most expensive operation in hospitals. By inference, it implied that emergency medical care is primarily responsible for consumers' mounting medical costs.

The same article also noted that emergency medical personnel are badly abused, working long hours under extraordinarily stressful circumstances. It also pointed out cases where people died or were maimed because of mistakes made by emergency medical staff. The article's message is that emergency rooms are both extravagant and dangerous.

The story apparently also produced editorial interest in markets across the country. In fact, several stories in other print and broadcast media can be traced directly to that cover story. The NATS leadership is naturally distressed and wonders what it can do to meet this barrage of bad publicity.

NATS contacted ProCom and said, "Do something." After a quick huddle, ProCom assigns you the task. Write a plan of action, then follow through with a news release about the plan.

NCCC 14 : 1

A former Dallasite, who is now a popular recording artist, has just gone public with a personal story in which she says recent bouts with alcoholism have been traced by psychoanalysis to abuse she suffered as a child. She claims she had repressed memories of being sexually abused at the Stemmons Center (NCCC's first site) by a woman she can only vaguely remember as Ms. Jones. She says the abuse went on for about three years until her mother, a single working parent, put her in a different child-care center closer to her new home.

Although she has not told this story before, it is getting wide play in the media because of her fame as a rhythm-and-blues singer. Within two days after this story broke, parents removed 16 children at the Stemmons location permanently. Other NCCC centers report some attrition, but nothing much beyond normal turnover.

Late this afternoon, three other adults came forward to say they were similarly abused by Ms. Jones when they were also clients at the Stemmons Center. NCCC management, immediately after the story broke, searched employment records and issued a news release that said no one by the name of Jones (or by any name similar to it) had ever worked at the Stemmons location.

NCCC did not deny the story, only that a person by that name had ever worked at the Center. NCCC promised to search employment records again. Later that evening NCCC told police it had found a record showing that an Evelyn Jossey had worked at the Stemmons facility for a period of four years in the mid-1970s, but that nothing in her record indicated anything irregular.

NCCC leadership is painfully aware of similar stories at other child-care centers in recent years, but it is unprepared to deal with the crisis. It called ProCom for help. ProCom passes the assignment to you. Thoroughly analyze the situation, and work out a plan of action. Then write a news release that explains the plan.

Independent 20 : 1

A national publication has ranked all universities, based on the quality of education and the treatment students get. Your university is ranked in the lowest percentile. The admissions officer has asked ProCom to help construct a student perspective on this claim. The publication making the claim is often used by parents and students as they begin searching for a campus home.

It is important for your university to provide clear, documented information about the campus and its education and treatment of students. This assignment has priority because the admissions office has already received calls about the story, although no enrollments have been canceled. What plan of action do you recommend in this situation? Once you've developed a basic plan, write a news release about it for the campus newspaper.

Notes

Appendices

Appendix A

The Standard Advertising Unit

The newspaper industry introduced the Standard Advertising Unit in 1981. The SAU was refined and reintroduced July 1, 1984. It is a simple system that defines a column inch as one column wide by one inch deep, where a column is 2.0625 (or 2 1/16) inches wide and there is .125 (or 1/8) inch between columns. Therefore, a 31.5 SAU ad can be 3x10.5 or 2x15.75 inches. By consulting the table below, a three-column ad is 6.4375 inches or 38.625 picas wide by 10.5 inches or 63 picas deep. A two-column ad is 4.24 inches or 25.5 picas by 15.75 inches or 94.5 picas deep.

The standard column width also helps newspapers use a modular page design. That's why only the widths and depths in the table below are recommended for modular-style newspapers. Of course, newspapers may accept ad sizes other than those in the table. For our purposes, use only recommended SAU sizes in all assignments.

Table of the Standard Advertising Unit (SAU)

All fractions are in decimals

Width in Inches	1 Col.	2 Cols.	3 Cols.	4 Cols.	5 Cols.	6 Cols.	DT
Inches	2.0625	4.25	6.4375	8.625	10.8125	13.0	26.75
Picas	12.375	25.5	38.625	51.75	64.875	78.0	160.5

Depth in Inches	1 Col.	2 Cols.	3 Cols.	4 Cols.	5 Cols.	6 Cols.	DT
1	1x1						
1.5	1x1.5						
2	1x2	2x2					
3	1x3	2x3					
3.5	1x3.5	2x3.5					
5.25	1x5.25	2x5.25	3x5.25	4x5.25			
7	1x7	2x7	3x7	4x7	5x7	6x7	
10.5	1x10.5	2x10.5	3x10.5	4x10.5	5x10.5	6x10.5	13x10.5
13*	1x13	2x13	3x13	4x13	5x13		
14	1x14	2x14	3x14	4x14	5x14	6x14	13x14
15.75	1x15.75	2x15.75	3x15.75	4x15.75	5x15.75		
18	1x18	2x18	3x18	4x18	5x18	6x18	13x18
21	1xFD**	2xFD**	3xFD**	4xFD**	5xFD**	6xFD**	13xFD**

*The 13-inch depth sizes may be used for tabloid sections in broadsheet newspapers.
**FD (full depth) can be 21 inches or deeper. Depths for each broadsheet newspaper are indicated in the Standard Rate and Data Service (SRDS).
Extrapolated from Newpaper Rates and Data, p. A14, May 12, 1989. Used with permission.

Appendix B

ProCom News Release (format)

ProCom Corporation, One Professional Plaza, Serene, USA 95959

Contact: Your name
             Your title

Phone: 123 456-7890 (office)
           123 789-8787 (home)
Fax: 123 456-8901
Email: www.procom.com

Date release was distributed   **For Immediate Release
(or insert imbargo date and time)**

Identifying head: Proper form for news release

Begin the body of your release about halfway from the top of the page. Use double-spacing. It's easier to read and edit. Take advantage of spelling and grammar checkers in your computer.

Be sure the contact information is complete, including your home phone number and the date the release was distributed.

If it is a timed release, delete the "for immediate release" line and insert the proper embargo information, such as "12 noon, Friday, September 7, 20xx." Be explicit.

An identifying headline should summarize the gist of the story. Its function is to tell editors in capsule form what is in the release.

-more-

(Some organizations number releases and put the number at the bottom of each page. It makes easier reference and retrieval.)

Appendix B, Continued —

Proper form for news release, Add 1 -

Use at least one-inch margins at the right, left, top and bottom. Indent paragraphs at least 10 spaces.

The first paragraph is the lead or summary of the most important fact(s) in the story.

Paragraphs should be short, preferably no more than four lines, punctuated correctly, easy to read and understand. Sentences should average no more than about 15 or 16 words.

If you are writing a broadcast release, use broadcast style. Especially remember to use active verbs, spell out numbers rather than using Arabic numerals and give phonetic pronunciation (in parentheses) for names or technical terms.

One-page releases are more likely to be printed or broadcast, but you can use additional pages as necessary. If you do, remember to insert "-more-" at the bottom of all but the last page.

At the top of the second page, flush left the identifying "slug" line from the suggested head and "Add 1" for page 2, "Add 2" for page three, and so on. Never split a word, sentence or paragraph between pages.

Although the symbol "-30-" is used most often to show the end of a release, some people prefer "end" or the symbol "###."

For releases sent electronically, put contact information at the bottom of the file to eliminate need for editors to scroll back to the front. When you send or take a disk, always enclose a hard copy. Mark the disk with the slug line, software used and your name, phone and fax numbers and e-mail address.

-30-

Appendix C

ProCom Radio Script

ProCom Corporation, One Professional Plaza, Serene, USA 95959
Phone: 123 456-7890. Fax: 123 456-8901. EMail: www.procom.com

Client:	Time:
Script title:	Writer:
Date:	Producer:
Page: of pages.	Studio:

PRODUCTION CUES	NARRATION

Appendix C, Continued —

Script title: Page   of   pages.

PRODUCTION CUES	NARRATION

Appendix D

ProCom Television Script

ProCom Corporation, One Professional Plaza, Serene, USA 95959
Phone: 123 456-7890. Fax: 123 456-8901. EMail: www.procom.com

Client:	Time:
Script title:	Writer:
Date:	Producer:
Page: of pages.	Studio:

VISUALS / PRODUCTION CUES	NARRATION

Appendix D, Continued —

Script title: Page   of   pages.

VISUALS / PRODUCTION CUES	NARRATION

Appendix E
(Letterhead)

ProCom *A Full-Service Communication Agency* ***MEMO***

1 Professional Plaza, Serene, USA 95959. Phone: 123 456.7890. Fax: 123 456.8901. Email: www.procom.com

To: Date:

From: Subject

Appendix F
(Interoffice memo)

ProCom *A Full-Service Communication Agency*

1 Professional Plaza, Serene, USA 95959. Phone: 123 456.7890. Fax: 123 456.8901. Email: www.procom.com